The
Kennaway Papers

The Kennaway Papers

JAMES AND SUSAN KENNAWAY

HOLT, RINEHART AND WINSTON
New York

First published in the United States in 1981 by
Holt, Rinehart and Winston, 383 Madison Avenue,
New York, New York 10017.

Library of Congress Cataloging in Publication Data
Kennaway, James, 1928–1968.
The Kennaway papers.
1. Kennaway, James, 1928–1968—Biography. 2. Authors,
Scottish—20th century—Biography. I. Kennaway, Susan.
II. Title.
PR6061.E59Z468 1981   828'.91403 [B]   81-47454
ISBN 0-03-059578-9   AACR2

First American Edition

Printed in the United States of America
1 3 5 7 9 10 8 6 4 2

To Denys from James,
to Rosie from Susan

TODAY IS JANUARY 5th, 1979. Ten years ago in December, a few days before Christmas, James died in a road accident. The car that James was driving had twice shot out into the fast lane of the motorway and twice slid back on to the hard shoulder. Finally it ran into the outside lane again and drifted slowly across the central reservation. He was struck by three cars approaching from the opposite direction. James's heart was crushed, but my brother-in-law told me that the coroner said that medical evidence indicated scars of previous damage.

It was concluded, unofficially, that James had had a heart attack and may have been dead or at least unconscious before the impact. It was also said that had James lived he would almost certainly have been an invalid. For some writers this might have been acceptable. For James, who lived his life at an orgiastic pace, it would have been intolerable. James was forty when he died.

My brother-in-law collected the few things that the police had kept for us, the most notable of which was a little red notebook which they had found in his pocket. James would usually write on anything: cigarette packets, telephone directories, newspapers, backs of envelopes, any scrap that came to hand. He also left a spiral-bound book, dated 1961 – probably the first that included 'diary' thoughts, in which he says:

Sudden determination to keep writer's notebook. Reasons? Apart from obvious one, that I can't get myself to write this afternoon, (1) That one's always losing scraps of paper. (2) That one's always wise after events. E.g.: I think I was very clever writing the script of *Tunes of Glory* considering that my views on the Army and all that had totally changed between book and film. True to my former self. When, foolishly, old man remembers, perhaps valuable to spot how one thought *then*. Perhaps repersuade oneself. No intentions, by the way, of writing Old Man Remembers but precedent shows writers tend to make mistakes of so doing. Reasons for not? (1) Evidence against one, if too private. Answer: won't be private: purely professional. (2) Release of tension into notes instead of play/novel, etc. Answer: will write first draft rough notes for piece, not separate essay.

On the very last page of the red notebook he had already written what he had described as the very last line of his book *Silence*:

There followed a bloody accusing and crying noise.

I wanted to start this story with his death but it was difficult to know when that episode began. I think perhaps it was in June or July of 1967. James had an arrangement whereby he exchanged a cottage near Fontainebleau in France with an old lady who, in her turn, used a cottage of ours at the Manor Farm House at Fairford. She was about eighty-five at the time and had been a friend of my grandfather's and was a most fascinating person. She loved James in an exceptional way and they enjoyed their time together. I did not often go with him because he went to work and when he was not working he talked to Helen and that was invaluable to him. On this occasion I had gone over to France in June, to collect him and to drive home with him in his new car. It was his birthday present to himself. He complained sometimes that he would be suspected of being a middle-aged lecher if seen driving too sporty a car; I suspect that the Calvinistic shades of his Scottish upbringing were actually responsible for these doubts. He believed in certain areas of self-restraint, or self-inflicted punishment; long gruelling runs that took the wind from him and that did nothing to reduce his weight; immensely long

8

working hours even when the inspiration was not at hand. In his list of enjoyable things to be denied he did not, however, include his absorbing interest in sex and women. He explained it as his right, an essential part of the creative process of his writing, a necessity. If he did feel guilty, he managed to subdue these feelings, so far as most people could see.

We stopped on the coast at Barfleur. It was a place where he stayed quite often; he loved the sea, and Barfleur, being on the north coast, was free of English-speaking visitors; cool, rain-washed, sea-washed; he said it reminded him of the clear air and granite of Scotland. At all events he went to Barfleur frequently and walked the sea wall in all seasons. The Hôtel Du Phare, where we stayed, was simple and friendly but on the morning of the Sunday that we were due to return to England by ferry from Le Havre, whilst I was in the bedroom packing, James walked into the room. His face was covered in sweat and, evidently in agony, he lay on the bed and told me he had a bad pain in his left arm and shoulder. He believed this was the result of an old injury which he had suffered many years ago when he was playing rugger at school. He had had a recurring back problem most of his life; one of the reasons in fact why quite often he stood up to write instead of continuously sitting at his desk. I really did think otherwise. I believed he was having a heart attack. It is ridiculous to say *now* that it was Sunday and we were in France and we didn't speak very good French and we didn't know a doctor and so we didn't see one, but James was stubborn in his disregard for medical attention. He had, after all, written:

Doctors, like mini-cab drivers, are the other idiots to whom we trust our lives.

Having lain on the bed for about twenty minutes, he seemed

9

to be recovering and he found he was able to move his left arm. I knew I should do something more positive about it but James had an unpredictable temper and I didn't want to upset him because I could see that he had experienced some very severe pain. So he said, 'Well, let's go out to lunch.' We had previously chosen a restaurant on the coast towards the seaport. His only concession to the pain that he had felt earlier was to allow me to carry the cases down to the car. He wouldn't let me drive. We arrived at the restaurant; I seem to remember it was rather like a greenhouse, a dilapidated place with steamy windows and flaking paint. It was perched on a cliff overlooking the sea. It was raining and windy and when we went inside the first thing he did was order us two large gin dry martinis. I think we both sensed that there was something really wrong but neither of us could speak of it. After a time he looked at me in his special foxy way and said, 'I think I'm going to make you cry,' and I said, 'I think you are.' He said, 'It would be funny if this were our last drink together because I think *now* you love me,' which was his way of admitting that the troubles we had experienced for the past few years were being replaced by a sort of happiness that at the time of the rows I had never imagined could exist. As the lunch was not ready we decided to go for a short walk and we climbed down to the beach. There were rocks covered in brown seaweed and a lot of dirty cans and wooden crates swept in from the sea, not a pretty shore. It was oddly desolate and smelling of rotting rubbish thrown up by the waves, but James was always drawn to the sea and he had written of the beach in Malibu:

I don't think I can be happier than walking barefoot down the shore, in and out of the edge of the sea, a literary beachcomber, poet manqué. I was thinking of the end of the world and all that, because impressed lately with Jung's dictum that the second part of life is ruined unless we are prepared to welcome death. This is of great importance, I'm sure, and while the tides still rise and fall I think I can manage the idea of death. But I'm afraid if the sea should grow still. If the sea's going to stop, then I can't bear death. Which is to say, cornering myself, that I, like every other person who has known happiness, believe in life everlasting. The mystery of infinity should itself reassure us. The waves come infinitely, infinitely. Life, and with it therefore hope, is everlasting. We are not cheated. There is no end. End is a term which we have invented, it did not exist, in the beginning.

On this occasion, however, it was different, not peaceful, but rather menacing. We were talking about the film *Psycho*, which I hadn't seen, and then we went round a boulder and there in the sand was the severed head of a grey horse. The milky eyes were open. It gave us a foul shock and the memory was with me for the rest of the day and brought an appalling gloom upon us as we hurried back up the cliff.

The one thing I did manage to do was to persuade James to agree to see a doctor the following day when we reached England and this he did, but his doctor, knowing how James hated any medical attention, really did not give him a very thorough examination and only told him not to worry.

Shortly before Christmas 1968 James was asked to do the script for *Wuthering Heights*, and he went to Yorkshire. He came back very excited because he said that for the first time he understood about Catherine and the purpose of Mr Lockwood's presence in the book. He now believed that Mr Lockwood was a medium and that Catherine was able to be seen and heard by him in a special way. To add to this he said that he felt that Catherine's plea to be let in meant more than opening the window to her. By knocking on the pane she was saying, 'Let me in, let me in to your hearts and to your imagination for ever by listening to my story.' He said he felt he had discovered something about the book that he hadn't understood before.

On December 21st he had to go to London to see Peter O'Toole but I asked him not to return too late to Gloucestershire as we had a dinner party. One of the guests was a French lady who had come to talk about the possibility of opening a restaurant with us. As she spoke only French, I thought his particular brand of gesticulation, phoney accent and charm would considerably ease the difficulties of the evening ahead. John and Tory Lawrence had been invited too, as it was hoped that Tory might become our partner. As we walked down the stairs to go to James's car I can remember quite well that he flicked his fingers up my skirt and said, 'So long, Crumb Bum,' which was a favourite quotation of his from Salinger's *Catcher in the Rye*. I went back upstairs and made the beds: he went on down and drove to London, in his bright new car. I did not see him again.

Later, when I had to face up to organizing the endless things that one must deal with, I had to go into his study and look through his papers and of course I found things that I did not know he had written. I had always known about his manuscripts because he wanted me to read them, or he read them to me at the end of each day. James used to say that for every slim novel that he published he would write an average of a million and a half words, which was not an exaggeration. The differently coloured drafts of each novel, which led from one to another, piled up in crumpled heaps under the windows and on every shelf in his study. Occasionally a single sheet would float from somewhere, spiralled by a draught, and settle on another pile, to add to the confusion. Many, many pages, many, many drafts had already been scrunched up by James himself, in the course of his writing. The trouble was that the character in the first book would become the character in the second book and the happening in the third book would reappear in the fourth or fifth, so it was extremely difficult to sort out one group of papers from another, one set of characters from another.

However, in going through these papers I found, muddled up with the fiction, letters and diaries which I had never seen before. I have to say that I threw away some of the letters that had been written to him because it seemed wrong at the time to pry into a part of his life that was not only over because he was dead but was over because we had, together, come to terms with it.

But one of these notebooks which I hold in my hand at the moment had, in typical James style, been edited by him twice, once in red ink and once in blue. He had written across the top of the first page:

P.S. March 1965. There seems no point in editing the note-book but of course it is of value to me now. One drawing has Susan's hand, otherwise the only foreign writing is David's in Paris. It flows through in this direction, ebbs on back pages; the flow as will be seen, is dullish except for a few fascinating indicators. The ebb's natural I hope, but I am putting red notes, or mean to some day, to help the stranger through.

At the top he put:

P.S. [and this is in blue ink as opposed to red] I guess the reader's trick should be not to *try* to read anything difficult unless it is in a passage that hooks him.

He also wrote in March 1965:

> One now begins to see why and when an author keeps a
> notebook and for whom, for people, for somebody, any-
> body who picks it up and reads. Why? Because his loneliness
> is complete. Here I have Rolf to talk to, of course, but there
> is such a backlog of material unshared, so what began on
> these pages as frivolous and ridiculous now becomes the
> most essential part of things. I guard this notebook in a way
> that I don't guard my passport. Where is it? (Oh, God)!

I put the notebooks in a box. I put the box in the bank. All the
papers that I thought were suitable I gave to the National
Library of Scotland. The Librarian came to collect them and
took them away and they have been looked after with great
care ever since. But it is now ten years since James died and
our children understand the nature of the crisis that occurred
between myself and James in 1964, and they also know David.
I would not want to publish this story if it were not that I
found in James's notebooks and diaries some of the best
writing that he has done.

When in 1978 I read Professor Francis Russell Hart's *The
Scottish Novel: a Critical Survey,** I decided to write to him,
for he had included a section on James. He was at that time in
Edinburgh on a year's sabbatical leave from the University of
Massachusetts, where he is Professor of English. He kindly
agreed to meet me and our daughter Jane. At the end of the
evening I hesitantly produced the diaries for him to read. It
was an impossibly demanding task that I was requesting, but
I needed advice and help. His initial reaction was similar to
mine. He wrote:

* Published in 1978 by John Murray

14

They do ASK to be read. His references to (I assume they are his) helping a 'stranger' read the diaries suggest that, for whatever reason, he expected them to be read. Interesting thing here: did he as a writer lose all sense of distinction between 'private' and 'public' writing – so that, at his most 'public' he was writing a fully confessional kind of thing, and at his most 'private' he had a sense of unknown and thus 'public' audience? I sense so. That in itself is a fascinating (and no doubt, for many people, a painful) development. Fiction, for him, I gather, came to encompass all fact, and fiction was 'dramatic', intended – if ever it was READY – for a 'public', a 'Reader'. At the same time, one feels that he was, in these materials, almost always writing TO or FOR himself, and the terrible loneliness of the writer for whom this becomes true is perhaps what compels him to expect and even hope for the 'stranger's' eye.

I hoped that Professor Hart would edit the diaries but he was already engaged on another biography. Other writers whose advice I sought said that it would be necessary for me to link the pieces together and explain the order of events. Perhaps at a later stage then, the material could be edited professionally for publication. With reluctance, approaching fear, I finally faced the fact that James would have expected somebody to undertake to work on the diaries and that I was the only person who could do that. The trouble is, James and I did not always see things quite the same way; so finally I thought it best that I should tell my own side of the story, not to justify my part in the plot, but to explain it.

At the time that James died we were on a wonderful 'up' and reading these diaries now makes me see what a miracle happened, because there was a time when I despised him so deeply that I thought no love could ever come again for us.

I was wrong; because for ten years hardly a day has gone by in which I have not thought of him, not always with sorrow. I have thought of his crazy ebullience, his wickedness, his introspection, his unfailing ability to surprise me, to make me laugh, to make me sad and to make me love. Above all I think I, and probably most of the people who knew James, will remember his zest for life and the way he entertained us when he chose to.

APART FROM JAMES and myself, the other person chiefly involved in these diaries is David. David had known my brother for several years and he was also friendly with my sister and her husband. In 1963 he came to London. He had recently published a very successful novel. He was staying with my sister and she brought him, one evening, for dinner with James and me in Highgate. Although our previous acquaintance with David had been slight, on this occasion James and David got on well together. All at once their shared experiences of writing and publishing brought them close. They were separate from the others.

In 1964 David asked James, or maybe James invited himself, to go to Paris with David to meet a film director to discuss David's latest book, which they were hoping to make into a film. For James, the visit to Paris in August was a shattering event. He enjoyed the company of David, the jokes, the adventures, the Paris life. He wrote to me:

I'm truly amazed by David. Believe me, he didn't get there by luck. The head is strong and the heart a much hunted one.

James took an instant dislike to the director. How much was professional jealousy, how much he felt that the director was interfering with the growing bond between David and himself, I do not know. He claimed that the director did not really like David's book and there were, apparently, big problems with the script. In any event, James was made to feel intellectually inferior, which was probably why he made up for it by behaving in a wild, wild way. He took it upon himself to show David the darker side of Paris and the darker side of his own character. He came home with many tales of happy, funny, outrageous and awful days spent together with David. But underneath, his confidence was shaken by the director's criticism of his own work and he was extremely depressed.

After leaving Paris, James and David drove up to the coast together. James was beginning to feel extremely ill. On his return to England it was discovered that he had glandular fever. My father, looking up the disease in one of his ancient medical dictionaries, quoted that it came from 'smelling noxious drains'. I remember giggling at the time, but of course James had such an attraction to the *nostalgie de la boue* that I think perhaps my father was not so wrong. In his diary he wrote and edited, in red, the following.

P.S. On way back through Normandy, already with glandular fever. Articulation, like adultery, is easy only for the thoughtless. That's why we write more slowly as we grow older and our earlier unthinking acts become unthinkable memories. You cannot for instance know the glory of sea bathing until you have a sense that you have sinned, until you are old, a sin in itself; then you enjoy in retrospect what you so lightly threw away.

And in David's hand:

JIM, you have done more for me in a week than I have done for anyone else in a lifetime.

Throughout the period that these diaries cover, James was always writing. He had started a novel, set in Kashmir, which he intended to call *Magnificat* or *Gorgeous Palaces*. Later he changed the title to *Maclaren's History* and transferred the setting to Scotland. Later still he moved the scene to London and by this time David had joined the list of characters. Although the book was fiction, he drew Fiddes in the likeness of David. This book, *Some Gorgeous Accident*, was eventually published in 1967. Link, in the same book, possessed much that was James.

Some Gorgeous Accident

A homosexual, or latently homosexual attachment, Mr Link? ... If I sometimes think so, Fiddes would go on, it is only because I can find no better explanation for such a close relationship. But perhaps it was just because we worked together ...

No, Dr Fiddes. It was not just because we worked together.

It was a lightning attachment. For one day, one morning to evening, you, Fiddes treated me, Link, like any other journalist arriving at the scene of the plague; gave me the distant English charm; the T. E. Lawrence–Dr Albert Schweitzer bit. The wrist-watch brush-off.

Once James's illness was diagnosed, there did not seem to be any treatment other than rest. He had appalling fevers and terrible dreams; nightmares. He would wake screaming and sweating in the night. He wanted to work but he could not concentrate; he was uncharacteristically unhappy and very weak. However, he did tell me some of the happenings of Paris and he told me a lot about David whom I did not know very well. He told me that the success of David's book, which was his third, had taken David by surprise and he was quite unprepared for it. David professed to need help with script-writing but I think it was probably only a way of making an excuse to get to know James better. David felt isolated from the people he had been working with and living with for so long. According to James, David's life had been extremely hard, unbelievably hard one might say, and he did not seem to be a very happy person. I think my strongest feeling on hearing of the things that David had told James was that I felt sorry for him because James's life had been so filled with excitement, even if he had made the excitement happen himself. David's life had been restrained by comparison.

Some Gorgeous Accident

Fiddes

Born: Seven years after Link. There's a scandal for a start.

Height: Two inches taller than Link. Outrageous.

Weight: Six pounds lighter than Link.

Waist: Three inches slimmer than Link. There were doubtless other comparable and vital measurements. Oh, but you're a loser, Link.

In life, Fiddes/David was only three years younger than Link/ James, and three months younger than me, but otherwise the differences were much as described above.

James had to go away for a brief period during the spring of 1964. David was staying with my sister at a cottage down by the river Thames. At that time James and I had a house in Fairford a few miles away. James suggested that as David might feel a little out of things I should go over, see how things were, and perhaps invite him back home. I can remember quite well driving over the fields; it was a sunny morning. A high humped bridge led down into the courtyard which was surrounded by a low stone Cotswold wall. There were groups of people in the garden sitting in deckchairs talking together, but there was one figure quite alone, apart, sitting on the wall, his arms round his knees, wearing a new suede jacket. The suede jacket was noticeable since it was the time when such garments were considered total luxury and even a successful writer who wore such a jacket was just a little bit suspect. I can remember thinking that he was wearing it almost as a sign that he was now a writer, an accepted writer, and that he did not care what other people thought, although in fact I believe that he did care.

When I approached him he seemed to recognize me with some relief as being perhaps an ally in a strange land. He jumped up and said, 'Let's go for a walk,' so we did and we spoke all the time of James. We moved around each other as in a formal, ritualistic dance, jealous I suppose of each other's experiences that had centred on James. But I did not allow myself to think too deeply why I minded. Later that day, or perhaps the following day, James returned home and seeing how difficult it was for David to settle comfortably with my sister's friends, he invited David to come and stay with us.

Our house was usually filled with children. Happily we had decided when they were quite small that we should take them with us when we travelled abroad. They had all been born in just over five years, Emma first, then Jane, Guy and David. We used to let our house in London and with the proceeds rent much cheaper accommodation in the less expensive areas of the Continent; usually out of season. Meanwhile, my father had let us his old house in Fairford at a peppercorn rent, as he liked us to visit him but not to stay; this arrangement suited us all. James liked working at Fairford, away from the wheeling and dealing of the film world and the pubs and clubs of Soho. Because the children did not go to school we were required by the authorities to provide an education at home for them. As we could offer a good deal of foreign travel we had little difficulty in finding young school teachers prepared to give the older children their lessons. I did the housekeeping but because each governess stayed throughout the year, ignoring normal school holidays and terms, each one inevitably became involved in the whole domestic life of the family.

Because the children lacked the companionship that those who go to school would normally expect, it was decided that Emma, who was very gregarious, should go to boarding school when she was eight. We wanted the school to be near Grandma, who lived in Perth and who would be able to manage outings and sweeties and new pairs of socks and generally deal with any emergencies, the thought of which threw James into a black panic. Eventually we chose Edinburgh and although James threatened to fly to Scotland every time he had a less than joyous letter from Emma, to bring her home, she eventually settled down to three defiant years of Scottish education. Jane joined her eighteen months later. So when David arrived in our house, we had only the boys with us, Guy and little David, and a pretty governess with whom David, encouraged by James, flirted not a little.

During that time we all got to know each other a little bit better, lots of jokes, funny voices, excursions; David looking in my cupboards, oohing and aahing at the tidiness; David telling stories to the boys, conjuring shillings out of their ears and generally making himself an extremely amiable guest. James and David were talking all the time, discussing George Orwell or Ortega y Gasset or the novel or the film, or just themselves. I did not feel part of these conversations but there were the children to be looked after, the meals to be cooked and I enjoyed domestic things. After a time David went back to the Continent and we resumed our life in London.

In 1963 I had had to have an operation that meant that I would not be able to have any more children. This probably affected James more than it did me. I had been so preoccupied giving birth and coping with babies for ten years that I had not been aware of much else. I was still very busy, but James used to say that the time that a woman spent having babies was similar to a moth in a cocoon. Sooner or later, when the babies grew up, the cocoon would have to be broken, and I think that he was trying to break mine. It is possible that he wanted me to be made more aware of the experiences that he himself had; to unblinker myself to his world. He was always determined to be responsible and so fairly cheerfully worked at films, which he disliked, in order to provide us all with bread and butter and pretty shoes. But it became apparent that he thought I should begin to live on my own account; to be involved in something outside the family; to find my feet in the big world. He wanted to prepare me for some nameless disaster. We discussed whether or not I should get a job or even start a restaurant. It seemed a possibility, especially as I had cooked endlessly and happily for years for all our numerous visitors both abroad and at home. But I didn't particularly want to do anything other than that which I was already doing and I couldn't see why he was pushing me so hard away from emotional dependence on him.

Perhaps in order to justify his own extra-marital excursions he would have quite liked me to have had an affair, and indeed so would I. The main problem was that I could not find anybody as attractive or entertaining as James and although I had been looking for some time, nothing of any importance at all had happened. James was a great manipulator of people. Many people seemed to think he had good advice to offer and many were foolish enough to take it, but he enjoyed playing with people's lives and it was inevitable that sooner or later he would need to begin to play with my life and with David's life and it was inevitable too the turn that that would take. The only mistake that James made was that I would actually fall in love with David. To complicate matters further I still loved James. I believe also that David fell in love with me and I know now that James and David loved each other in the way that David and Jonathan were brothers.

Some Gorgeous Accident

Link's love, his speech, his actions, why even his thoughts had overtones of violence; of pain experienced and pain inflicted purposely. He was a man who arrested attention and invited passion with dangerous facility; dangerous because, as he welcomed life, seized it by both hands and pulled it in the door, he let destruction in as well. His eyes were bright, but not large. The lines on his face looked as if they might occasionally, nocturnally bleed, and were his smile ever to have been caught aptly by a painter, then viewers of the completed head-and-shoulder portrait would have been tempted to say, 'That man Link must have a club-foot; or a hump, maybe; or even a withered hand ... ' And in the end, serious people did not sympathize with Link because he had guts or humour (or even the writ of a private soldier with a soul) but because they marked in him what they perceived in every cripple: a creature they felt first repulsed by then drawn toward; namely, that naked, cornered, confused and humiliated child: self.

Link had evil's illegitimate quality, its pure beginning, its ironic regret, its obscenity, vitality; but not its self-knowl-edge, not its 'no' side. Link still loved Link; which is to say that he still had a private, savage appetite for life.

'Whereas,' he would have started his story's theme, 'whereas I loved this other one like a brother; a younger, sadder, if no more serious brother ... '

they had a great thing going. Two loners, two egos; well matched, ill met. Link trusted Richard David Fiddes; maybe the only one he trusted altogether.

Here was a bond of egos proof to any sly, atavistic gambits of ids: a friendship with a tacit promise flung in the teeth of dismal, amicable experience; similar to and not detached from man's most solemn will to love: freely to live.

...

So he wandered over to the old woman. Link went too. Fiddes did not seem to mind; even seemed to expect him to follow; talked to him as if he were a close colleague. They were like two men going a long journey over narrow planks, Fiddes leading the way. When they met, there were always the same ironies, obscenities, insults and jokes. They spoke to nobody else, at least to no other men, in this way. Two in a league apart, to do with life and death, not 'Let's arrange a dinner with the wives,' or talk of income tax: two conceited guys.

I suppose it is not too difficult for me to write about what happened next because I seem to have no sense of guilt. This could be for two reasons; one because, as I said before, James meant everything to happen that subsequently did happen, except for the part that hurt him, and secondly his own behaviour had been such that every time, or almost every time he had an affair of any importance, he would tell me about it. It was a sort of therapy for him. Frequently when he got blocked on a passage in a book and didn't know how to approach the paper on the next day, he would promote a ding-dong between us. He would take me out to dinner, he would start to needle me, I would refuse to respond, not wishing him to know that he had succeeded in hurting me, which was his objective. A good storm. I would be too kind, too understanding, but eventually he would make me angry and we would finally have the most blazing row. He would go to the study, complete the chapter and I would go to bed in raging tears. For James, this was the sort of stimulation he needed in his daily life and I think that quite soon, when he could not get the stimulation that he required from me, he would seek it elsewhere, so that the whole system became rather overworked.

Some Gorgeous Accident

But that was never how it went. Work, orgy, bend, crisis, explosion and work. Be careful now. Don't start hating Link. Don't start hating the Linky presence, Linky legend, Link.

There were very few episodes that he did not tell me about and indeed very few infections that I did not catch on account of his way of working. But he usually did not tell me about the affairs precisely when they were happening, and by the time he did tell me it seemed extremely pointless to break up a marriage for something that had happened a month, a year ago and was by now over. In any event, he never disclosed all, certainly not enough to dislodge me from my domestic shelf. Of course I was jealous and angry and my pride was desperately dampened but our marriage was exciting and special and a great deal better than any of the marriages that I saw around me.

There was one episode in his life which nearly caused an

end to the 'wedding', as he would call it. That involved the French Canadian woman whom he met when he went to Ontario in 1962. He had hoped that Michael Langham, who was the director at the Shakespeare Theatre, would be able to produce his play *Country Dance*, which was taken from his novel *Household Ghosts*. However, upon his arrival in Canada he became violently ill and was put into an isolation hospital as the authorities suspected that he had brought some Asian disease with him from India, where we had all been living for several months. In fact his illness turned out to be mumps. James was in hospital some time, lonely and depressed, but when he came out I suppose he wanted to see if the rumours about men and mumps were true. However, since the virus had not travelled lower than his neck he had to be fooling somebody, even if it was only himself.

Then he met Anne. You will see in the extracts that follow that David's wife was called Ann, so to avoid confusion, I have spelt them differently.

James told me a little later about what happened. I think the relationship was passionate and violent, probably containing the fiery ingredients that were lacking in our own relationship. As a successful documentary film director, Anne was able to meet James and stand up to him on his own ground. Despite James's high hopes, the play did not seem to be progressing, so perhaps he took his disappointment out on Anne. He stayed in Ontario for several weeks and then they moved together to New York. He described to me the fierceness of their lovemaking and the stormy rows which set him in such an excited spin. I know that he considered the possibility of staying with her, but despite his need for a more mature person than myself he decided, after three months away, that he would leave her and come back to England. I do not know if he saw her ever again, although there were letters between them.

I never met his French Canadian Anne but I do know that the experience he had with her was very important to him and it certainly shook me up a great deal because it was the first time it had occurred to me that he might have left me for another woman. It was because of this episode that I too thought it was a bad idea that I should be so dependent upon him. In my own way I tried to withdraw myself so that the hurt, if it should come, would not be so terrible. He had been, up until that moment, the only person in my life that I had lived with or loved. However, much as he wished to make me independent, at the same time he seemed to need 150 per cent of my mind. He thought I was withdrawing because I was upset about the sort of life that he was leading. I was in fact, I suppose now, withdrawing in order to protect myself.

One day, soon after he came back from Canada, he went out and left a letter for me to find on the kitchen table. It was unforgettable. Written on yellow paper, it frightened me so much that I at once tore it up (I later retrieved it and glued it together).

I found the pressure he was putting on me to love him more and even more at total odds with his declared interest in other women. So I could not appreciate the intensity of his feelings towards me and felt overburdened by the responsibility that he expected me to return this love in the same bright coin. My immediate instinct was to separate myself from this claustrophobic love, to find a quiet space between us. This is the letter that he wrote and that I now believe was the catalyst of future events as far as I was concerned.

Dear Susan,
We must not drift apart. Peculiar physical circumstances merely emphasize, or precipitate, a crisis. I have insisted on

mentioning other women; your reading of such indis-
cretions is that I am giving vent to forces of destruction
within me, destroying you, lest I destroy myself. But all I
have been trying to say is that the women are symptoms,
not of course a disease. They are irrelevant, immoral etc.
à la Perry Mason.

Within me certainly (particularly thro' Anne whom I did
my best to destroy) something extremely destructive has
exposed itself. I know this as well as you, I must have faith
that something equally creative is beginning to compensate
it, and I hope and trust first signs of this will 'happen' in the
new Indian novel.

My impulse at the moment is Gauguinesque. In every
cruel action to wound you, especially when there has been
no compensating bed, I have demonstrated a clear desire to
exchange the responsibilities of art. No man is born an artist.
Various strains – and aspirations – make him one. Fantastic
concentration and selfishness – I have watched it in every
living artist I know – bring him to his goal. You have
understood this in a way I could not reasonably expect. But
now I have the feeling that you are suffering, badly, in the
process. I am terrified that I am destroying you. But if you
truly understood me you could say 'silly mistaken boy' or
'true artist' but you could not be destroyed. You are precisely as dear to me as life itself. We joked, years ago, and
in jest we found the absolute truth. You are my white horse,
you and our children. There could never, never, never be a
replacement for that. I see you, each month that passes, more
not less of an angel and that is what disturbs you. Understand therefore that I commit no cruelty to you which is
not properly directed at myself. You are precisely as dear to
me as life itself. The rest is a nightmare or a dream. If you
were to fall, I would maybe continue to write but I would

not continue to live. I have only lived through you. Had I been satisfied to be a publisher we would be the happiest couple in England. Unless you understand that you are, precisely, life to me, we stand to be the unhappiest. I can explain no better than that. Withdraw and I will perfectly understand. Withdraw, and you kill me. I know of no love that has been tried harder, and proved true.

See you.

J

When I first started to work on James's diaries I decided that I would not write about David and what happened between us. The book was to be for James. But then I realized that there was so much that I could not account for without explaining a little about our love. I had known James for a long time before I gradually fell in love with him but with David it was different.

In November 1964 following James's visit to Paris, David arrived in London again and came to stay with us for a few days. Because James and I were supposed to attend a dinner dance on that first evening and because David had not brought any suitable clothes, James devised two outfits from one suit. David 'steeled himself to the alien crutch' and wore James's pants and a velvet jacket. James wore the evening dress jacket and a pair of rather worn blue trousers. They were a splendid pair. They spent the evening joking and secretly sending up our hosts and devising ways of how to beat 'the system'. I did not dance with David until the final obligatory goodnight waltz.

I had always been slightly envious of the girls who attached themselves to James and attracted his attention by talking of their problems. I thought, 'How marvellous, here I have a conversational gambit. I will talk to David about my problems,' and that was how we started the dance. When I told David that I was seeking a small revenge upon James, it had simply not occurred to me that David could be in the least bit interested in me. His attitude up until then had been nothing but brotherly; perhaps he thought I was the permanent faithful wife. So it was to my amazement and excitement that, in the spirit of a grand flirtation, we finished that dance. None of us seemed to want to end the evening so we made our way to a nightclub where we met celebrating friends at the door. They decided to join us but in the smoky darkness we were unable to find a table large enough to accommodate us all together. I remember James arranging for a couple of girls from the club to join the party too, but David and I found a separate table some distance away, and I knew perfectly well then that we were heading for more than a flirtation. The way he looked at me and called me 'Susie' and the way he held my hand was too serious. That night at the dance I experienced a sudden and absolute thump of excitement. My mouth was so dry that when I smiled my lip caught on my teeth and I was aware that David felt the same. It was the first time that I had felt this way and I could hardly believe it when David expressed the very same emotion. We had arrived at the same point at the same time and what followed was inevitable. I never considered the rights or wrongs, it was just like coming home. It seemed so natural that caution was unimportant between us.

In the nightclub we talked and danced and on the way home we sat in the back of the car and held hands, secretly. James had drunk a lot and was a little quarrelsome. He went to bed. David and I stayed up and talked. When I finally went to bed I could not sleep.

I woke up in the early grey light and went to the little girls' empty nursery. I stood by the window. On a clear day you could see Epsom Downs. Then David came into the room and we stood and watched the sun come up over London. So far as love was concerned, we seemed not to have a choice. There was no need to pretend or waste time with coyness, but as we saw no logical conclusion to this astonishing happening, we had to be reasonably cautious so far as the rest of the world was concerned. Having decided that, we had only to find the time to make the arrangements to be alone together. I cannot remember how I stumbled through the rest of that day, bewildered and upside down, but I do know that the three of us went to the cinema and saw *Jules et Jim* and in the dark I sat between the two and each held my hand. Even then, if I had been asked to relinquish one or the other, I do not know which I would have chosen.

Deception is never pleasant, least of all to write about, but then it seemed quite right that David and I should arrange a poste restante address so that he could write to me on his return to the Continent. We managed the odd telephone call whenever possible. I went down to Bond Street and booked myself a course of German lessons so that I should be able to leave the house if he were able to come over; and I did not have long to wait. Shortly before Christmas David arrived and asked me to find an hotel. I left the house early, cancelled my lesson and we spent the day together. In the evening, after I had left him and returned home, James met me by saying that David had just telephoned from the airport on his arrival in London and that he had invited him home for dinner. I drank so many martinis that I had to go to bed early. I felt I was missing many precious moments but could not face seeing David and James so comfortable in each other's company. The following days were hectic – it was nearly Christmas and I had the shopping to do and all the preparations for the holiday. David and I met whenever we could, driving round London in my little green car, visiting the Tower of London, meeting in the crowded Christmas shops. I always seemed to be wearing my tartan scarf, my polished black new boots and long coat to match. We drank martinis and had tea at the Ritz.

David knew perfectly well the sort of life that James had led on the side of our marriage. I think perhaps he had been quite shocked, but he never used this knowledge to his own advantage. He never discussed it with me and must have thought my deliberate blindness to be extreme innocence; but of course the unspoken comments on James's infidelities clearly helped us both to make our own decisions.

David came back to London again after Christmas while James was away. He visited me at the house and played with the children and we went out together again on every possible occasion. We really didn't talk about the future because we were so happy with the present.

JAMES AND I had decided to take a house in Austria for the winter and spring. Our arrival at Zell-am-See was typically chaotic. I had been taking those German lessons in London so that I could see David on his brief visits to England, but also because I did not know even basic German.

On approaching the house agent in my faltering but, I considered, grammatically perfect Berlitz German, he had shaken his head in uncomprehending stubbornness. James wheeled in and flapping his hands, speaking pigeon Italian in a German accent and gesticulating towards the snowy mountains, persuaded the clerk of our identity and destination. I was quite mortified but grateful and we laughed at James's success. Once up the mountain our confidence collapsed. Of all the places that we lived in abroad, the Haus am Berg was without doubt the gloomiest villa we had ever seen. It was situated on the side of a mountain with an icy track leading up to it, where the car frequently slid over the edge and into the ditch. The windows were small and overshadowed by a heavy roof. The boiler in the cellar might have better suited the *Queen Elizabeth* steamship; the furniture was dark and heavy. Into this house we eventually settled, James skiing early in the morning before the sun got up, as was his habit, so that he didn't enjoy it too much (shades of Calvin), and spending the rest of the day working.

David and Ann were living not far away in Vienna. James, the manipulator, invited them and their little boys to stay with us in our awful villa for a few days' skiing. We met them at the station and took them up to the house. There was not even enough hot water to bath all the children, although hilarious hours were spent stoking the boiler. The children were more or less of an age, all blond heads together at the table. Ann was pretty, quiet and introspective. In my joy at seeing David I had not anticipated how hard it would be. We managed to lag behind on the ski slopes or stay shopping in the town, but these were only brief moments and all at once even kissing had become a furtive pastime. Out walking together while the children, running ahead, tumbled in the snow, I began to see that either we had to be stupidly brave and go on, or stop seeing each other altogether. Love was becoming too painful. Whatever I felt for David, which was a completely new experience in my life, I knew that I still loved James and I hardly considered the possibility of leaving him, let alone hurting the children. If divorce was not an idea that I had ever entertained in connection with the things that James had done, I certainly did not entertain it now. On the other hand I did not see how I could possibly survive without seeing David again.

The little visit finally ended. It had not been a great success. The children quarrelled and cried a lot and only James seemed to be enjoying himself. It was with a mixture of relief and agony that I waved them goodbye at the station.

Although David was living not so very far away, in terms of communication things were very difficult. Before he left we had decided that we would not want, nor be able, to break up our families so that we two could live together. But I suppose I hoped that from time to time we could see each other again and that I could refresh myself with David's love and care. Living with James was rather like being a moth caught in a lighthouse lamp: the glare and intensity of his attention could be terrifying. It was fun but it wasn't the sort of peace and contentment that I was looking for then. David and I were foolish enough to think that we could make do with a meeting here and there, from time to time, hello and goodbye. Having said goodbye, the only way that we had left to communicate was by letter, and James unfortunately found one of these letters.

When James found the letter that I had been writing to David he was so angry that I hardly knew his face. James had previously arranged to have lunch in the town with me, the children and their governess, but when we arrived to meet him, the hotel we had chosen was closed. He was waiting for us in a terrible temper and for some time I thought this was because the arrangements had gone wrong and that he was frozen waiting for us in the cold. We eventually arranged to eat in another hotel, and it became evident to me during the meal that there was something seriously amiss. He would explain nothing to me, but his eyes blazed hot and sharp. It never occurred to me that he could have found out about David, so I agreed to drive up to the house with him after lunch, leaving the children to struggle up the icy road behind us. His anger was extreme, his bewilderment quite alien to him. I do not believe that he had ever been jealous in his life before. His instinct was to run.

When he went to the house to collect his things there was one very bad moment; he could not find his passport. He had packed in haste and thrown his bags into the car. He was half-way down to the town before he remembered the elusive passport. I meanwhile had remembered the green insurance card which was necessary if he was to cross the border. I had it in my hands as he came storming up. He did not realize that I was intending to call him in order to hand it over. In his fury he believed I was attempting to conceal it. He accused me of preventing him from leaving and then demanded where I had hidden his passport. My mind was a total blank. I had no recollection where it might be. Helplessly I watched while he tore the house apart. It was eventually found under the table-cloth in the hall, where he himself had concealed it for safe keeping. There was no doubt in my mind by now that James must go, though of course the minor inconvenience of being stuck up a mountain without a car did not occur to me then; and that, subsequently, was the least of my worries. He took all the money too. I later discovered that he drove to Italy where, when we had first started living abroad, we had rented a farmhouse in the hills behind Alassio.

This was where he returned to recapture the memories of innocent sunny days. He drove furiously up and down the Riviera, trying to find various friends of ours whom he thought might give him support. But most were not at home or did not want to know, so he resorted to letters and telegrams, which arrived at Zell in very fractured English. This made them extremely difficult to understand. I felt too shell-shocked to respond with much feeling and I certainly had no intention of begging his forgiveness. I did not, after all, feel that I had done anything so very wrong and although I was prepared to do almost anything for the sake of peace, I felt very obstinate and rather angry that he should think that there was one law for himself and another for me.

At another time and in another place, James himself put this collection of telegrams and letters together. The reference to the 'idiot wife' is from Graham Greene's *The Complaisant Lover*. William was our solicitor, whom James was pressing to start divorce proceedings. As the telegrams were always late arriving and often in the wrong order and as he had usually tried to telephone as well, I had great difficulty in sorting them out. If he was confused in Italy, I was confused in Zell.

Cables

Area Verona. 12 midday Friday 5th Feb. '64

Kennaway to Susan

I CAN'T SEE HIM AGAIN PLEASE I NEVER WANT MY CHILDREN TO SEE HIM AGAIN I CAN'T LOOK AT YOU WHILE YOU ARE SEEING HIM I WILL RETURN THURSDAY P.M. YOU GO DARLING IF YOU

38

MUST GO THURSDAY A.M. WITHOUT PUBLICITY PREJUDICE OR POST MORTEMS AND RETURN OH PLEASE RETURN WHEN YOU WISH BUT ONCE AND FOR ALL PLEASE COVER EDINBURGH OUTING ALONE REPEAT ALONE DARLING NEVER FEAR TO RETURN TO A LOVE THAT MAY BE HOPELESSLY IMPERFECT BUT IS TRIED IS REAL TO ME IS AT PRESENT FEROCIOUS AND BROKEN HEARTED BUT REMAINS AT BOTTOM AS SUNNY AS GARASSINO AND WILL AGAIN AND AGAIN BE NEW INFORM JEAN THESE DECISIONS HOW I SMOKE VERONA NOW HOTEL DIANA (ALASSIO) OR HOTEL LAIGUEILIA TONIGHT. LOVE LOVE – JAMES

In Alassio. Thursday morning a note from a mutual friend Mrs Olivia Morris who lives here, 'Telegram from Susan':

CAN YOU FIND JAMES HOTEL LAIGUELIA OR DIANA ALASSIO RED CITROEN T.T. PLATES PLEASE TELL HIM LETTER POSTE RESTANTE ALASSIO MY TELEPHONE ZELL-AM-SEE (AUSTRIA) 2897 LOVE SUSAN KENNAWAY

Sunday midday Kennaway to Susan

AT ANY AND ALL TIMES IN MY LIFE I WOULD HAVE ANSWERED MY LAST CABLE TO YOU BY MY PRESENCE OR VOICE NOT YOU THEREFORE BE GONE USE MANOR TAKE OR LEAVE GUY DAVID ARRANGE BOILER STOKED UNTIL MY RETURN THURSDAY CONFIRM EDINBURGH TRIP HOTEL DIANA UNREALISTIC IDIOT RETURN ONLY ON KNEES OTHER DESCRIPTIONS UNPRINTABLE KENNAWAY

Received on Sunday a.m. Alassio:

Susan to Kennaway

RECEIVED INCOMPREHENSIBLE TELEGRAM BY TELEPHONE NO

39

COPY UNTIL MONDAY MORNING SENT TELEGRAM LETTER POSTE RESTANTE ALASSIO DICK* SENDS THIS FOR ME WILL GO EDINBURGH WILL RETURN LOVE

On Monday morning the delayed letter telegram was received from Susan to Kennaway:

WILL GO EDINBURGH THURSDAY BUT WILL RETURN FOR GOOD IN ONE WEEK IF YOU WANT ME THEN LOVE

To which on Monday morning Kennaway replied to Susan at 11 a.m.:

IDIOT DENTIST'S WIFE STOP WILLIAM FULLY INSTRUCTED STOP OBEY PREVIOUS TELEGRAM STOP SO LONG CRUMB BUM KENNAWAY

Such confusion, and the telephone calls were not much better, what with the long waits to place a call and the hopelessly indistinct lines that existed in those days.

Letter to Susan — from Hotel Diana, Alassio

Tuesday 9th – after 'phone

My darling, darling, only love, I am still too shaken to trust myself to more than a few words. As always there seem to have been ten misunderstandings a day, I don't know if you yet understand: I took your telegram on Monday morning to be the *letter* of which you'd spoken so thought you'd replied to mine simply saying 'I'm going off with him'. But

* My brother

40

it's over; I can't quite believe it. I dreamt I was murdered last night, but we seem to emerge. I don't think anybody did any wrong, which maybe proves I'm insane, but if I am, I know the reason is that I have only one hold on the world, only one connection to reality left and it is you and I thought you had gone away. When that happened my heart was so evil that it passes description and all love was hatred. There was only barren anger and destruction left to me, and I thought perhaps you'd never loved me and the world became a random cheat and farce. I intended to kill him, maybe you ... Oh, God, it all smelt of sick. And then your letter came.

I love you. I think only of having you again gently in my arms. I can't believe it but there's a stillness now. Don't weep any more. You are loved, loved, loved. Only rest, and please gently nurse the possibility of opening your heart again to me. There will be no failure, ever, in my response. I'm not so old. There is, I promise, a whole future waiting. For your mother there was none. For you there is, there is, I swear: I know.

love, my pretty only love,

James

Letter to Susan

Wednesday

My darling:
I'm writing this in the same room, 5, north of Verona where I spent the worst night of my life. I am not so foolish as to expect that there are no bad ones ahead. I honestly don't

think they can be worse, because you must understand that when you handed me my green card I thought you had asked me to leave you forever. I believe I struck you. And I loved you then as I love you now – each step more since I first took my eyes off Jane Meredith and Mieke Wyatt,* obsessions at one time. Because I'm so muddled and (proved) unreasonable I'm trying to stop myself writing fully till I have your letter, but as you have never for one second, night or day, been out of my brain how can I stop myself putting something to paper.

First since there was such a muddle, I *beg* you to come inside my head (I, of course, am on my knees, not you, but I realize that as I send it) and get my sequence clear.

(1) At noon on Thursday, six days ago (25 years after I buried my father, to the day, very important, he'd been much in my mind) I amble upstairs, get some paper since I told you to, a written piece falls out, my eye catches my name and 'getting back to the old life' – I think 'I shan't read her novel', then, flash, 'your poor Fred' flash '3rd letter since … ' I'm perfectly calm. I read no more. I think well, well, the sly bastards. How smelly of them.

(2) At 12:30 I meet you and realize I can't look you in the face. You ask me 'when did you discover' (meaning Blue Post Hotel closed) twice and against my own better judgement I say (lying, by the by) 'about two months ago'.

(3) We have a reasonable talk in which you say only one thing 'couldn't you go with Anne'.

* My great friend

(4) Of course I relive three months in which I really really truly have been trying very hard to get you closer. I also relive David's friendship and every scene makes me a cuckold and a fool.

(5) Everything began to tremble for me and all that I had built up, all the effort and in my odd way work-wise the integrity seems taken away. You say 'obsessed by him'. As I rage and rant, I see your face cold, cold to me then rattled shouting 'You must have David', then the passport and I know that I am thinking 'where is the kitchen knife?' and that I am insane. And I feel a fool, a fool; because there are no rights or wrongs. That you should be with him is my failure. I wonder if it was my physical failure, my failure in your eyes as a writer – 'You're the better writer' you said. I hung on that.

(6) I drove here. Morning crawls in. I send a telegram. I feel won't ever bring A. Karenina back, but it seems right to shout. I ring Mark* who says 'Remember, James, you haven't any grounds to stand on', and I suppose everybody must say James is a hopeless husband. And I think, maybe. But Susan knows, knew everything, really. And I drive of course, I relive the previous evening, the previous three months.

(7) I have to race to Alassio at a terrible speed to get to the Telegraph Office before closing. Nothing, Doctor, my heart's broken: I heard it. No one to blame except yourself.

(8) Next day nothing at the post office. I walked familiar

* Mark Longman of Longman's Green

ways, drove towards Florence, drove back, thought maybe she was never in love with me. That's the irony. She has been pure angel, I ludicrous, but all the time it was I who loved her and lately she has talked of always knowing something would go wrong, of not going to the grave having fucked only you (you unsatisfactory bastard). Relive, relive. And now I suppose he's come from Dublin and they're in each other's arms.

(9) Self pity no way of going on. I must survive. There is a plot afoot, a plot of the Gods whereby everybody in my life for nearly a year has been set to destroy me. I have an enemy, I know what to do. I did love her, always, I am guiltless on that whatever 'rights/wrongs'. People say I know this to be true, and if I'm guilty now, then to be fair she must have been in some way guilty before. I never never never would have refused a call from her like I sent yesterday ... A message from Mrs Morris. *Letter* on the way ... letter? Of course, she's gone with him. 'I hope this doesn't inconvenience you too much.' *Susan* would never be so cautious with me. He's advising her; on the way to her; with her it's war, war, war. And the purpose of battle is victory. The only victory left to me, seeing she ignores me, seeing she saw me at the end of my tether weeks ago, since she doesn't open her mouth or her heart to me, then there is only one victory left, I shall hurt her; then maybe kill her. I know the breast where I'd put the knife, I like her body now, better than ever, I want her always on bare feet on these sands ... You are going insane Kennaway. Send telegram and write William. Fuck hanging about. You will not be destroyed. Fight, hurt. Telegram and letters (I don't forget the woman who spent £1,000 in anger, freeze the joint account).

(10) Sunday. I love her. I want to go to Ortovero. I can't I can't. There is no spot on earth, my earth which she has not touched. All the time she never loved me. And I have loved her so that the only other one who ever loved with me – perhaps the only one who loved me, I think then – driven to nervous collapse yelling 'Damn Susan, Susan, this Susan, why will you speak of Susan?'

Fight, Kennaway. I can't get through to Anne. I write and say all is in chaos. I will write again. But the moment of truth is about to be ... As I post it, I know the moment of truth has gone by. If Susan leaves, I'll work, work here. I'll book an apartment through the man at Sandi's. Invited Mrs Morris, don't go. Susan would have gone. Do something Kennaway, you'll go under. I go to Ventimiglia. So this is truth. There is no Susan. There is no audience for your books. There was no Garassino. My children were better dead. Now I will certainly kill. But first we'll have all the evidence – cable William, act promptly on my letter – cable Susan, you want war you can have it, you want to destroy me, you won't: not until I have taken you by the throat, have opened your mouth and have killed you stone dead, you inadequate love-refusing Brief Encounter absurdity. Die, die, die. And him, though I'd better use a gun there.

The children? Well, my Pappa hopped it. Why not me? So long as one of them gets the idea of what love is some-time, I'll have done something – Does she not know that had she given me herself wholly I could take her to eternity in a way that none of my friends – none, none, none can understand? But of course she doesn't want that. That's where you're wrong. That's not allowed in marriage. Passion is a word that's gone ... But I will hurt her any-way. I'll spoil the soppy honeymoon ... William rang.

Everybody's upset, good. I tell him they're all good liars, half of them trained that way; be ruthless, ruthless. There is only one outside chance left. That I am right, that I alone am mad maybe, called mad certainly, and in reality; that my passion for her is right, is, is, whatever happens and somehow find R. Neame* in grand new villa. I explain, describe. His face is grave. I've lost you. I know ... I go half way home to Alassio am now certain that I'm going under, can't she understand the profundity of one love against another? No, I about turn and go to Nice, fuck a big tart called Babette in a brothel and give her all my money. More than usually meaningless. Evidence for Susan. Oh fuck that. What I want of Susie is too much (damn that 'Susie') that's one trouble, I see it, it's sick, the yellow paper letter's right, the truth is that I'm a madman asking Susan not merely to love me but to keep me sane. That's sick, sick, poor girl. His love is healthier for her, much, even if it doesn't begin to have the depth (like his books, thanks, hang on to that) – He is interested in other people; he has an audience; he is sane, gentle, shrewd, wanting love and society. You've asked for something no human being can be expected to give, that's what's wrong – nobody, nobody, not even Susan twigs you've made yourself a cuckold making absurd and excessive demands on her soul. All this love was in your head. Everything's in your own head. Fight Kennaway fight. You must eat.

(11) Fuck up with the Post Office. Her telegram – no letter, therefore she must have meant this telegram says 'I'm off, will return in week or more if you want me then'. Ha ha, Beauvoir, what balls you write. I would have easily forgiven, but I cannot, cannot – and she must see that – let her

* The director of *Tunes of Glory*

46

go and come back, this might dawn on her. If you go it alone on your books for Christ's sake, boy, don't give in now, go it alone on a love that I've never seen approached – and I look – in this decade on this earth.

Her letter arrives. Grave? Grave? Stave? I can't read her writing. I can't believe it. There's a glimpse. If she gets 'grave' couldn't she get it all, couldn't I build again? I can't believe. I ring. Confusions. Connection. The voice of collapse. Good. The voice of innocence? I can't believe that, I know man – know myself too well. The letter 3rd in a day was it? Of course I can't – collapse. I've heard it before. I'm a madman. She should go with David. I ask too much of her, much too much ... Yet I want to believe, how I want, want to believe: don't dare. I'm terrified at the possibility that my life could begin again. Mind you, Kennaway, you won't be destroyed, you won't, finish the book. I get drunk. When did I eat? Sleep, sleep.

(12) Mark shouting at me that I'm a shit, get down on your knees, chum, and pretty quick. You don't understand. I never said right or wrong. I haven't thought of divorce, only tactics to give pain, because I am not afraid to hurt directly someone I love, as I curse myself for hurting indirectly. I didn't say that because I knew, knew he couldn't understand. I love *Susan*. Why is this such a sin? Why all get at me about children, this, that and the other – Of course one can fix them. But even Susan makes a sin of loving too much ... I'm mad. She ought to go with David. She'd be happier then, more normal, and he's heaven I know. Therefore make up your mind now, Kennaway, to tell her, 'Damn David for his mildness, go with him, go, quick'. I love *Susan*. It's not an act. It's a fact that explains every bloody act in my life. Why must I be told it's a crime? On

the 'phone, the first realization of hurt comes across and I'm stunned – but if she were in my hands – Susan's talking of running off, dreadful telegrams, week's peace – But of course. Yes, yes, anything always.

Obsession, David, of course, I see it. And good on him, by the by: apart from one cynical bullock necked Mulligan,* he seems to be the only one to have noticed that you've become the best woman in Europe. I mean it. And such a rest that would be for you, in the end. I realize everything is still in turmoil. But if you re-read that yellow letter (which I can't remember in detail) and did not resist, my darling, because my weakness, my madness, my terrible unhappiness – I'm damned if I'll say less – is that you won't risk the journey and there is nothing of which to be afraid. Somewhere, right behind, you have never trusted that love so of course it has been abused. I'm maybe mad. Make up your mind: I love you, Susan. Listen and dare.

xx J

To Susan

Alassio 1964

Susan, compared to him I know I have nothing to offer, because I have nothing, nothing to offer beyond my love. But, darling, when you think – and here's grounds, unnatural demands, all that – can *you play* with *him* scenes played with me in Mr Browne's villa on Lake Whatsit – there was true respect by the by, and Susan was there then and in Florence,

* Mick Mulligan, the jazzband leader

48

no blaze? And tell me do you think that Anne and you were all that different, with regards to repressions and ideas of love, when you both set out? To Hell with the children, darling, that's next, my teeth are in your bowels, to stay. I love you beyond comparison, beyond belief – I swear – in sweat in blood in birth in death, oh, darling, I want you barefoot in the sands again, mature, not as you *were* or *might be*, but as you *are, are,* darling, darling cunt, as you are with children yelling off-stage – and I'll show you paradise.

I must stop. Goodnight, my soul. My very soul.   x

Letter to Susan

I love you, Susan. Whatever you did, whatever you do, I love you I love you. I love you. Therefore feel no fear and guilt is part of tragedy not comedy. Life is for living.

James
xx

This is an unposted letter found in the diary, written while I was in Scotland seeing Emma and Jane at school, written to Anne in Canada.

Anne darling,
As Gemini, as well as everything else I hope you'll write me soon. The crisis prolongs itself; continues from pain to more pain, through passion and coldness, random and misunderstanding and often I wonder about Anne. The hell I've created now around me, moving *everybody* (she, him, friends etc.) can only be compared to the hell I created with you in New York and to have the second woman crying

'James, you're a destroyer!' a woman of the same kind of incredible strength as you – makes me tremble, tremble; know that I cannot, must not yet appeal to you. Anne, all hell is loose, and yet I'm not that; I swear I'm on the right side. Everything between you and me is out, by now: I mean 'is known to Susan' and really I don't know whether I've half destroyed for you or you for Susan. My mind tells me I've lost you both – yet can't believe it: my heart is torn in two, like hers now, like yours. Yet is it fair that I shall have to live without either, having so carefully trampled on you in order to preserve what now seems to be beyond preservation – Susan and the other four, dear heads?

Anne: listen to me: bear with me: in your thoughts take care of what I am to you. Because I have never before been afraid and am now afraid; need you desperately: must not call for you, yet, if ever. I shall call, if I call, once, definitely, utterly and forever. Meantime I contrive here alone at Haus am Berg, Zell-am-See – one of my children involved in a horrifying accident, with a car. Oh God, oh God – the number Zell-am-See 2897 if you can ring, but soon I must get out, go South and I have friends near Nice so please cable or write to Poste Restante, MENTON, Alpes Maritimes. Darling, you must decide whether you tell your husband everything or nothing meantime, but I'm already reaching out a hand which you *must* not refuse as friend even if not as lover, because I would never refuse you such. I seem to be a Svengali. I'm not.

James was still in Italy when the time came for me to return to England to see Emma and Jane for their half-term. It was a long-standing arrangement and one that I was only too pleased to fulfil. I dreaded James's eventual return to Zell, so I thought it best to go before he arrived. The governess was able to bridge the gap with the two boys in my absence, but I had no way of telling whether James's feelings would cool down before my return. There was nothing very reasonable about James. I was frightened, not of James's anger or his threats to divorce me or separate me from the children, but by the idea that I might not be able to see David again. David had written to me at once with such love and support that for a short time, even though I knew it was not what we had planned, I felt that there might be some chance of a life for us together. But neither David nor I had imagined the wildness of James's passion or the sort of fight that he was prepared to make in order that I should stay with him. There were few weapons he did not subsequently use to break the spell.

I decided, at David's suggestion, to travel back via Vienna. David sent his secretary to meet me at the station, where I arrived long before dawn. I had spent the journey sitting wide-eyed in the empty carriage, but although she kindly took me to an hotel I was quite unable to sleep or even drink a cup of coffee. I needed just a few minutes with David, to say goodbye which, in the event, was all we had. David had an interview that day but he took me to the airport and we repeated that this was to be our last meeting. David gave me his pen. I remember making a fool of myself on the aeroplane. I could not stop crying. The stewards were solicitous and clearly thought I was having a nervous breakdown. Once at Heathrow I took out my purse to find a coin to telephone my friend Mieke. I dropped it and the pennies rolled away. One or two of the passengers who had observed the scene on the aircraft came forward. They dialled the number and hovered helpfully until I had made my arrangements. The following day Mieke and I flew up to Scotland together. We took the little girls out to lunch and then returned to London in the evening. At the airport a reporter came up and started to ask me questions.

Mieke steered me away with a few tough remarks over her shoulder about people minding their own business. I didn't want a scene, I never wanted a scene again. Scalded by the unpleasant encounter at the airport, I returned to Mieke's house to find a telegram from David saying goodbye again and that he still loved me. But if seeing David and the families together at Zell had convinced me that they should not be damaged, then, that day, seeing the girls, reinforced my resolution. I felt I must go back to James and really try again.

Some Gorgeous Accident

This was an obsession which made a nonsense of sleep. Not that Link suffered from insomnia: the opposite. When he wasn't listening avidly in Court, or talking compulsively about the hearing, in the pub, he slept all right. Snored, the bastard. But he dreamt unceasingly, so he claimed, of nothing but the other two. Told Clarky on some Bloomsbury pavement, 'That must be love; some sort of Machiavellian love, that hanging hate. They never leave me, lawyer. Their problems hook me up, follow me to the shower, come between me and the yoghourt left in the carton. I wake wondering what problem it is, about them, what angle of the insoluble triangle that I'm supposed to solve. The data floats away. The hang-up is left like a cloud over every day.'

'Take a sleeping pill,' Clarky said, putting on his bowler hat so it touched his bunny's ears.

'Nope.'

'Be a good fellow. I'll miss my bus. I told you before, Jim, you make a life out of stirring it up. You blow on your own dramas, and that's not a good thing. That's a pointless thing to do.'

Granted, Link felt: they only say, 'Don't take any more drugs' to those who are crazy with dope.

While I was in England, I spent a miserable time trying to decide if I had enough courage to return to Austria at the end of the visit. We had a friend, Denys, who was due to come to Zell for his skiing holiday. He had been at Oxford with James. They had shared rooms for two years and Denys had been James's best man at our wedding. I felt I had to explain the situation to him; I thought he would probably cancel his holiday. But he didn't. Instead he was wonderfully kind and understanding, which I had not expected, as I had felt him to be more James's friend than mine. He promised support and gave encouragement and arranged to travel with me back to Zell. We arrived there in early March, a little like nervous mourners at a wake.

On our arrival, however, James was absolutely charming and it seemed, briefly, that he was going to allow the whole affair to blow over. But he couldn't let things alone and with Denys there to talk to, he drank too much, got far too angry and the terrible rows began again. We had so many scenes, so much pain and tears and anger and anguish. James was used to me being a fairly quiescent person; now I was raving and shouting too. In a ghastly way he found it stimulating and was beginning to enjoy each new occasion. He was getting the reaction he had always wanted. But then, over-reaching himself, he had the idea of calling David to Zell-am-See to discuss the situation. When he first asked David to come I don't believe that he had thought out any special reason, but apparently the idea occurred to him that since he loved us both he would try to do the right thing and make us both happy. Looking back now, it seemed he didn't want the drama to end just yet and was setting in motion acts to complicate the plot still further, so that he could write a better script for us.

A number of things went wrong with the rendezvous that James had planned for himself and David at the station, on David's arrival at Zell. Instead of arriving back at the house with David, James came with a case of wine that David had sent by rail as a 'thank you' for the skiing holiday. James half suspected that David had organized the wine instead of himself, but it happened to be a confusing coincidence. James decided to go back to the station. It was getting late in the afternoon and I thought David was not going to come. But then from the window I saw him in the snow, on the other side of a high wire fence that ran down into the valley. I went out to him in my slippers, through the snow-drifted garden, but we could only touch hands through the mesh. David, having decided to have an unbelievably severe haircut on the station at Vienna, had missed the train. He then arrived at Zell by the next train while James was bringing up the wine, and thinking that he was not to be met, decided to walk up to the house. Taking a short cut, he had landed up the wrong side of the high wire fence. After I had finally managed to get him over the top and he had tumbled into the snow, we trudged together up to the house like prisoners. Denys considerately left David and me alone for a few moments before James reappeared at the chalet.

Arriving back from his abortive trip to the station, angry as he was, James was nevertheless pleased to see David and rushed to the case of wine, popping corks as if it were Christmas. It all seemed so friendly and jolly.

Some Gorgeous Accident

'Nothing's changed, has it, Link?' That's what Fiddes' face said. And Link's smile was warm.

'Of course not. Nor ever will. You're my partner. No women, no war, no God can break that up.'

And Fiddes was glad about that: Link was his only friend.

James had started the evening at an impossibly high fever, laughing and joking, being as ebullient as he had ever been. Denys, David and I were muted in comparison, horrified at the act being played before us. However, I don't think it was until we were all having a meal in the town later that James finally formulated his plan. The idea came to him that the only way he could make David and me happy was in fact to give me to David. Towards the end of the evening James began to discuss the actual details of the transaction: the arrangements; train timetables; packing; had I remembered my passport? The bizarre joke was becoming a reality and it looked inevitable that something terrible would happen before the evening was through.

James had had a lot to drink, as indeed we all had by this time, but he was not so drunk as not to overlook the fact that David did not readily accept the gift that he, James, was about to bestow upon him. Clearly it would have been extremely difficult for David to take me anywhere at such short notice and at that particular time. James, sensing that there might be an opportunity here for him to make more problems, did not hesitate to point out to me that David was not as willing as he might have been. He stood up abruptly from the table and claimed he would not, could not pay the bill and that David would have to do so as he had more money than James. James then grabbed Denys and they left the restaurant together. I was stunned and unable to decide what to do. If I left with David, it would mean leaving the children and while I knew that James could neither morally nor legally separate us for very long, they were such an integral part of my life that it seemed an impossibility to leave them at all. We did not even know where James and Denys had gone. However, Denys then came rushing back to say that he had James ensconced in the bar at the station and that there was still a train in about an hour's time. He offered to help me walk up the hill to pack a few clothes, which I did in hopeless haste, and then we returned down the hill, slipping and sliding all the way, I clad in unsuitable shoes and 'going away' clothes, to the station bar. It was here that Denys and I discovered James and David talking to each other, old chums, old friends, comforting and swearing and laughing and crying all at once.

Some Gorgeous Accident

Meaning, Fiddes?

Meaning, 'How can you blame me? You told me to grab. You told me that life was for living. You told Susie too. You brought us to this – not that we're doing anything. You breathed on us your boozy, acrid, smudgy breath and we must have found in it fresh air.'

Meaning, 'Nothing has happened, Link, don't add two and two to make five. Except of course you're right. I love her. I love her more, by the way – to judge by all you've told me about Furstental, about all those things – I love her more than you do, Link.'

But, meaning too, 'I'm not betraying you, Jim. I'd never do that. If you're worried about all you've told me, that's absolutely safe –'

...

Susie picked her way through all the young doctors and

56

nurses who looked so like young actors and actresses playing parts of doctor and nurse.

'May I join you?'

'Sure,' Link said, and Fiddes asked, 'What can I get you?' Neither seemed too pleased to see her. Poor Susie.

Nor did they make it too easy for her after that.

The two of them talked over her head while she sat and drank by a tiny round table that had maybe come from some ship. They talked of Mandy-Margaret of course, and her attitude to authority, even when called to Court. They went on then to talk with enthusiasm of the Chairman and his big book; they were excited to find how close their observations were when Susie, rightly, couldn't take any more.

By this time I think James felt that he was winning the evening, but he could not resist calling out to me that I should be ashamed of myself, leading a young man like David by the nose; which was hurtful in the extreme, as the one thing that I felt I really knew about David was his love for me. It did help, though, to determine my feeling for James, which was nothing short of hatred. The 'nasty wee Scot' was fighting and since David did not put up much of a spirited defence on my behalf, I got fed up and went outside and tried to find a train to fall under. Unfortunately Denys came out too and hauled me back and eventually said to James that as David and I had now missed the train, we had better reshape the evening's pro-gramme. It was at this stage that we found ourselves out of the bar, shouting and screaming in the lobby of the frozen station, creating an appalling scene. James had one of my arms and David had the other and they pulled in opposite directions; God knows why, because neither really wanted me by this time. James howled like a banshee and Denys eventually dragged him away. Too horrified to make any sort of decision,

David and I slunk off round the corner and cautiously found somewhere to stay for the night. During that sleepless cold darkness I never for one moment imagined that I would be leaving Zell-am-See with David in the morning.

It was, I suppose, with some relief, while we were drinking our coffee, still early in the morning, that we saw Denys come into the hotel. Shaking the new snow off his shoes he said, 'You'd better come to the house. I think James is going mad.'

Of course I knew that that was what David had wanted to do all along, and that is exactly what we did. We climbed the hill again and we went into the big bedroom, where James was curled on the bed in his vest and pants, unshaven, in the foetal position, crying. It had been snowing in the night and the white flakes piled up high against the window panes caused both a strange lightness and a shadowless gloom in the room. David went straight to the bed and sat across the end of it. 'Old Jim, old chumbo, old chum, come on,' he said, and James peeped through his fingers, and their conversation began. I walked out of the room and I knew then that my little affair had ended.

Some Gorgeous Accident

Link was at the fixed-in modern bar with Clarky and maybe he'd already swallowed one or two. The idea of the dinner-of-departure had been entirely his.

'Sure, doc,' he'd said, over the phone. 'You want to get right out of town, maybe Brighton, somewhere like that. Brighton's only an hour. You can come up to Court for the winding-up tomorrow, but hell, poor Susie, she needs a break from all this.'

'Probably needs a break from both of us.'

'No, don't say that, doc. She loves you. I told you. I always said this one could be your Furstental.'

'Jim, if it really hurts, if –'

'You deserve it. Both of you. I'm not kidding you. She really has been kicked around too much. And she's confused. That was obvious in Court. Jesus, this Major Barbara bit … Isn't she just like every other pretty girl? She gets some idea into her head, goes to all kind of lengths to prove that this crazy image she has is her real identity. Then Graff comes in for ten minutes, says, "Dear, don't worry about your identity, you're a goer anyway, so quit lying about everything –"'

Fiddes interrupted, 'I'm not sure I saw it quite like that.'

But Link got the giggles.

'Oh, doc,' he said. 'You too. Quit lying that you understand about her. She's confused with knockers, with a switch-off and a come-on and a famous pappa. Now don't give me that you see her any deeper than that. That's a sight further than Turgenev perceives, in love … Listen, doc.'

'I can't listen all night.'

'You certainly can't, so you get round to her; hound out of here for the night. There's a train south every hour. But before you go, don't be slinky, don't give me the creepy treatment. Not that you ever did. You've got style, doctor. Sure you have. I'm in the bar here with Clarky, specially so we can give you a good dinner, maybe wave you on your way.'

'Jim, is that –'

'Sure, it's how it should be. This isn't a divorce, you know that. This is quite a separate kind of case.'

So Susie got dragged along, reluctantly.

She didn't want anything to eat, but agreed to a large

Scotch. They all sat down in the corner of the lounge, for this uneasy wedding breakfast.

'Susie, I think you should have something to eat.'

'No thank you.'

'But the bride –'

'Jim!' Clarky said, in the voice he usually used for his dog. Then Clarky engaged her in conversation, asking her polite things, about the Boltons, who lived in Number 10, and all that. She played along.

Link told Fiddes, 'You should eat. We should have a big scoff then away you go. And, Jesus, it's a while since I've been on the town.'

'Avoid the gymnasiums,' Fiddes said, looking a little less like the widowed groom.

Link took it well, said, 'Maybe. And another thing. We're doing good here, we're really beating this silly old triangle thing. I'm glad you're going off. Glad I pushed it that way –'

'You pushed it?' Susie asked fiercely, then looked at Fiddes.

'Oh boy, but she's beautiful,' Link said.

Fiddes grinned, 'And the guts.'

'And the tits.'

'Jim –' from Clarky.

'And the guts,' Fiddes said again, looking her in the eyes, so she melted just a little.

'And the pants,' Linky said, meaning about who was wearing them. But Clarky talked of other things.

Later, two or three drinks later,

Fiddes and Link were giving each other a blow-by-blow account of Mandy and Graff. Analysing the Chairman's mood and the home life of the man who had neither rod, staff nor mace ... They were really enjoying themselves while Clarky engaged Susie.

Then Susie suddenly whipped round and told Fiddes, 'There's a train in five minutes.' He didn't look happy, at all, about that.

She prompted him again, almost shrewishly:

'At nine forty-five.'

Fiddes looked at their drinks.

Link wasn't laughing at all. He had grown very pale, as if he were furious with Susie. Had she been with him and tried to break up a party like that ... Oh boy.

But Susie didn't look his way at all.

It was as if she had blinkers on. She stared and stared at Fiddes until he said, 'You'd rather take that?'

'There doesn't seem to be much point in waiting. I've no appetite.'

'No.'

Fiddes looked ashamed. Smiled faintly at Link and Clarke. Susie behaved as if she'd been married too long to him, or perhaps as if she were ten years older; and too used to having her own way.

'Does that mean we're going?'

'If that's what you'd like.'

'That is what I'd like.' She got up, walked away from the table, saying a brief good-bye to Clarke but nothing to Link, who grew even paler, leaned back and watched Fiddes as he followed Susie. Watched his fingers as he moved them in a faint little bye-bye wave.

Link's eyes then fell to Susie's boots for an instant, before she disappeared from the room. Clarke moved round beside him and poured him another drink, out of Susie's abandoned glass.

Link said, 'Christ, she really does want to pull him on.'
Clarke said, 'Take a drink.'

Link said, 'Jesus, that common little tart. Just to get up and go like that. That's rude. She looked awful. She'll certainly be the ruin of him. And I was dreading this moment of departure. Even her legs looked bad in those boots.'

It's no good pretending. Link was even worse than that, going on:

'Clarky, it was too easy. I see it now. I've been kidding myself. This is a big revelation for me. I've been kidding myself. I don't love that girl. I've felt I ought to love her. Been scared to admit until this second that I'm not hung up on her at all. Seen her for exactly what she is, a common little bourgeois Jewess, who's going to get what she wants. What a way to go. If that's how you say good-bye to someone who's loved you off and on for five years, then my God, is it good riddance. It's all over. Everything.'

...

Susie cried. She went straight to a bench nearby and began to tremble and shake and weep. Fiddes sat beside her, took his hands from his pockets, put them on her shoulders and said, 'Darling, if it's no good like this –' So she sobbed more violently.

'We're puppets,' she said. 'We're the puppets of that bloody bastard Link.' He tried to comfort her. Maybe taking a leaf from Mandy's book, she swore at Link again. When she paused and looked round the station there were very few people there and she didn't quite believe in it.

Clarke and Link then arrived on the scene and the couple stood up, hand in hand. Link roughly grabbed her spare hand, pulled her and said, 'You're coming home. Come to your senses, woman.' All his remarks might have come from a retired major, at this point.

Fiddes didn't let go the hand she held so tightly in his.

Link said, 'If you'd stop leading poor Kildare by the nose and – '

'Jim, I don't think that's fair,' Fiddes said.

'You close your mouth,' Link told him. Then he jerked Susan's hand and arm very hard so it hurt and tried to draw her away. Her sobs rose to a little scream. She broke free and began to run. She ran to the first platform she saw. There was a train moving out. She was past the barrier before the ticket collector could stop her. He was still trying to call her back when Fiddes also rushed by.

...

Susie smoking. Susie with a set expression, a bright-eyed, ruined, hating, glum look which said, 'He brought me here, believe me. This is one move I didn't make.' She sat on a chair at the end of the bed as if she had been brought to visit a man sick with a disgusting disease, of which she still had no fear. Brought to a deathbed, perhaps, of some boring and ancient aunt whom she had never loved or respected. Most likely Link's tears made her turn her head away. And Link didn't like them either.

'It could be,' he muttered, 'that we're witnessing the end of Link's love affair with Link.'

'We're back,' Fiddes said.

'Where did you go?'

Fiddes tried to laugh. 'God knows where that train went,' and looked at Susie who stared back at him with resentment. He unbuttoned his grey coat, put his hands in the pockets and sat at the end of Link's bed. Link looked tough in his vest, with a night's greying growth on his jowl.

He said, 'I let you down, I guess.'

'*You* let me down?' Fiddes said.

'Sure. I let you both down. Let me down too. That's it.'

'Oh no, Jim.' He even touched Link's ankle through the blankets.

'I tell you, yes. I set it up. I gave it the grandiose touch, the big gesture, and the moment it came to pain – old stuck-pig Link, you bet.'

'It wasn't a good idea.'

'I tried – '

'Not one of Link's best.'

'I really did try, doc. I know you love her. I wanted to do the right thing, and I – '

'And you went mad. It was just a bad idea. We twisted the triangle once too often ... '

And so on.

Interrupting each other. Don't be ashamed. Of course I am ... let you down ... Cigarettes ... So they did not even notice when she left the room. Probably Fiddes saw her go and thought she was about to take her coat off: something of the sort. In a way it was tactful of her; he could apologize more sincerely and openly, could persuade Link, carefully, that he had lost nothing. Could rebuild the old Linklove-Link. Because Fiddes was a very nice man.

HAVING STARTED THIS story with the last few years of James's life, I realized that I had become obsessed with the picture of James as he was then and had almost lost sight of the James that I first met in 1949. The James that I never knew before that date I know a little about now, because I have read some of the letters that he wrote to his ancient cousin Edith and I have read stories and poems that he wrote when he was at school. I have also seen delightful photographs of James, an earnest, kilted, studious little boy with short hair and a rather anxious expression.

When in 1940 James's father reported for an army medical and was told that he had only six months to live (and indeed this turned out to be the case), James began to take his responsibilities towards his mother and elder sister very seriously. He told me that as the only male in the family, he was aware of his position. He wanted to be the dutiful son, and up until the time his mother remarried, they had an extremely close and happy relationship. He certainly seems to have tried hard to please, both at home and at school, and I think probably the first major disappointment he caused anybody was when he decided to opt for history and English rather than for the sciences. It had been hoped that James would be a doctor, as was his mother, but quite early on he writes about the plays and stories with which he was involved at that time and he says in a letter to his mother in 1956:

I wonder sometimes if you realize just how much my writing matters to me. I have to be poetic about it as it does not claim to be anything more than entertaining, but I feel very strongly that there is hope there.

On leaving his school in Scotland, where, of all rather surprising things he had won the Cadets' Belt of Honour in the

O.T.C., James entered the army for national service. Once again he threw himself with great zest into the training, although he had never considered the army for a career. After two years with the Cameron Highlanders, spent mostly in Germany, sporting his kilt with a swagger amongst the *fräuleins*, he went to Oxford to take a degree in Politics, Philosophy and Economics.

It was at Oxford that I first met him, on a sparkling May morning. He arrived, uninvited, on my doorstep bearing a crate of champagne and a box of Black Magic chocolates. Alas these gifts were not intended for me. He had fallen violently in love with short-sighted Mieke, with whom I shared two dishevelled rooms in St John's Street, round the corner from the Ashmolean Museum, where we were supposed to study art at the Ruskin. She myopically and continuously failed to recognize him in the street and he began to visit me in the evenings to consult how best he might win the much sought after and very fair lady.

I had come to Oxford via four unhappy years in southern Africa, where my sister Gyll and I were sent to live with my mother's oldest sister, at the outbreak of war. I was just ten. My aunt was a spinster lady, eighteen years older than my mother, and she lived as a governess in Rhodesia. She lived with a family who were also friends of my mother's, and all the time we were there we thought their having us was an act of charity. We did not discover until many years later that our father paid all our expenses and more. It was an uncommonly austere household, my aunt was extremely strict and we were desperately unhappy and unloved. Our parents, once having made the arrangement, seemed content to leave us there. We did not receive many letters. Our ex-chauffeur wrote quite often, but we had few other letters and no family news. After two years we were sent to school in the Union, to Johannesburg. That was our happiest time.

At the beginning of 1944, in desperation, my sister and I had had to arrange our own journey home from South Africa, feeling that we were never to be recalled from our hated banishment. We appeared shortly after D Day (unannounced and unwelcomed on account of the censor), hotfoot off a troopship, wearing lipstick, high heels and unsuitable colonial clothes. If we had longed for, and expected, the loving warmth of our mother once again, we were to be disappointed. Our parents had divorced while we were away but no one had told us. Our mother had joined the Polish army and was working in Scotland and our father had moved to the country. Daddy surveyed us in shocked silence and then telephoned Cheltenham Ladies' College. Bewildered by the grimness of the English girls' public school system, I soon longed for the sunny country that I had once so much despised. My plans to return and to become a nurse were thwarted by my father's decision that I should go to Oxford. He hoped that I would catch a decent English husband. I suppose, because of the prim restricted life we had led in Rhodesia and the inhibitions and fear imposed by school in England, by the time I reached Oxford in 1948 I was shy and insecure. James chatted away and pranced around me on his knees, howling like a dog, wagging an imaginary tail and gazing at me with spaniel eyes. Nine months after our first meeting, he invited me out to dinner, on November 5th, 1949, and I fell in love.

James was secretary to the Conservative Association and edited their magazine. He occasionally spoke at the Union. In general he was a very sociable person, an outgoing spirit. It was with great delight and joy that I re-read his letters a short time ago; letters written to me during our holidays from Oxford and every other moment that we were not together, love letters, ebullient and tender, which took me straight back to those amazing days.

My very darling Susan,

I am listening to Mr Attlee making a very personal attack on Mr Churchill, and I see no reason why I shouldn't write a very personal letter to you – but by no means an attack. Today, I met a man who in September is trying – for the fifth time – one part (not 5) of the Bar exam. He didn't give me much cause for optimism, and I retired in disorder to the National Gallery – where I learnt a great deal. I then had lunch with Mother at the Lyric and we dropped in to see Nancy Mitford's translation and adaptation of Rousseau's exceedingly improper – and it is improper – play, *The Little Hut*. Robert Morley was glorious, and so I enjoyed it enormously, even though the theatre was half empty.

And all the time, more and more, inevitably, increasingly, irrevocably I adore you: adore you for what you are, not for what I take you to be. Adore you for all your silly fears, and irrelevant thoughts. Adore the thought of your coming to live with me, here and constantly; adore you physically, because now I have no desire to learn my way about any other woman. I want now and always, to find my way about you, to learn every intricate, delightful inch of you. I want to see your eyes, to hear your laugh, to dance with you, and eat with you, to find joy and overcome crises with you, to turn half through the night and hear your sigh, feel your breath on my face, the comfort and excitement of you, against me.

Believe me, sweetheart, I find waiting harder, or selfishly, I hope equally as hard as you, my adorable Susan.

Love you, now; love you forever,

James

Curse that sinister organization, the G.P.O. for delivering this at breakfast time.

I was at once back at Oxford sitting in his room or in my digs, or going to a party with his friends, having coffee at Elliston's or doing any of the day-to-day things which filled our lives. I could even remember the clothes that he wore; usually rather old-mannish and belonging to his dead father and smelling of mothballs. I could remember the conversations that we had. Nothing very remarkable. The most remarkable thing was the fact that this was a very different James from the one that was being revealed in the diaries.

He worried about getting a job so that we could get married when we both left university, and he was also very concerned about his writing work in progress at that time. In addition, he decided to sit for the Bar exams, having tutored himself. It was a long shot, but one that quite appealed to him. His father had been a solicitor and he was currently enjoying the charge of excitement to his system which came when he had a slight success at the Union. Since he enjoyed working himself hard, he found it a pleasant challenge. Needless to say he failed the Bar and was not at all disappointed. He had had one or two short stories published in quite well-known magazines, and while I think it never occurred to either of us that he would become a full-time writer, certainly writing was occupying more and more of his life. However, at that time he did not need to feel the loneliness that was later a prerequisite of his involvement with his work. We were a very ordinary couple. He proposed to me during a dance at a country club, in the minstrels' gallery, and in due course, when he could afford it, he bought me a ring. The engagement was announced on St Valentine's Day, 1951, and we were married in Oxford the following October.

James succeeded in securing the job that he most wanted. On leaving Oxford he started working for Longman's Green, the publishers. He worked on the scientific and educational side as an assistant to John Longman, one of the directors. He enjoyed his work immensely and in the evenings, when he came home and at the weekends, he wrote. By the time that Emma was born he had succeeded in publishing a long short story, 'The Dollar Bottom', in *Lilliput* magazine, which gave us enough money to buy the layette for the new baby and a domestic boiler for the kitchen. He also bought a ridiculous amount of very expensive French scent which he brought to the hospital and which rather embarrassed me in front of the other patients, because of the wild extravagance they clearly suspected.

He was also working on his first novel, *Tunes of Glory*, which was published in 1956. We were both stunned by the happy reception the critics gave the book. In a way I think James rather regretted this success because he had not found the book difficult to write and while his agent and his publisher and his friends would urge him to write another novel in the same vein, nothing was further from his ambitions. He wrote in his diary in 1961:

> *Tunes of Glory* (novel) proved only, to me, that I could characterize, i.e. write.

He added, incidentally,

> *Household Ghosts,* that I could feel. Trying now, (very dicey) to show in *Settling Down*, that patchily, I can think. *Country Dance* is, I think, a refinement of 'I feel' and beginning to believe that I like to go to the theatre to *feel*, unlike others who like to think. In books I also like to *feel* but don't actually sick up at a little thought here and there.

He wrote to his mother a letter, in September of that

70

year, which he never posted. I found it in his notebooks.

The strangest thing is that I should have turned out such a serious writer. I'd be best advised to stick to lighter stuff from the bank manager's point of view, but there isn't the same achievement. We can lower our sights later when we need bread.

It is becoming more and more ludicrous to pretend that the point of my life is anything other than writing. All the day and half the night I think of nothing else. For days on end I am totally immersed in the work. Where it will lead, except to megalomania, it's hard to see, but the facts have to be accepted. The curse of it is that it gets out of hand. The only way to get away from the difficulties one's encountering in the work is to live hard, nearly to blaze, to drive places quickly, see things, do something else intensely. Then it all relaxes and one broods and everything becomes vaguely unsatisfactory and one wonders why the hell one is living this way. One's living more intensely than most people but the equation doesn't equal happiness; then life doesn't equal happiness; pain and danger is part of it, always have been, and ever shall be.

The other thing, and I am not at all sure if this is in the least connected with writing, is the sense of brevity of life. It undercuts practically every decision I take. Whether I am a child of the times here, or whether seeing a father die young hurried me along, I don't know. I have no faith in the morrow. The idea that I shall see my children grown up is immediately, automatically dismissed.

Yet life's far from miserable. Indeed I am enjoying it more now than I ever have; then we have a natural instinct to love life, nor does the thought of death worry me immediately. It would disappoint me. It would be awkward for some others and embarrassing for the bank. The family, one worries about. I suppose it's just an occupational disease, considering life and death. Just now I want to blaze, in every direction, right or wrong, just so as I shan't sink with too much left undone, too much never tried, too many sensations missed.

I don't suppose I'll post this now. Quite often I jot down nonsense addressed to you, then it strikes me that it might worry you, so I leave it. There is nothing to worry about but there are facts to be faced. I have changed quite a lot. I've remained a child, more of a child than before, even, in some directions; and in others I've outstripped my contemporaries. I suppose I'm what is called an outsider now. No team spirit, no society in the accepted sense. A lot of amusing acquaintances, a handful of friends who are becoming less not more close, neither English nor Scottish, nor richer nor poorer, uneasy.

But God, how much better it is than being with the 90%; than being a potato. One should count one's blessings, even if it implies one's conceit.

Love James

Much influenced by the *Notes on the Novel* by Ortega y Gasset, James was beginning his great change. Occasionally he would have to travel abroad in the course of his work at Longman's and I recently read the letters he wrote to me then, still love letters, passionate, writing of his intense loneliness whenever he was away from home and his overwhelming need to be with me and with the children.

By 1959 we had our four children and we moved to a house with a view. The garden was full of old apple trees and blossom and sloped away down Highgate West Hill. James was hopelessly undomesticated. Although he had small, exquisitely shaped hands, he couldn't hold a screwdriver, mend a fuse, fix a dripping tap or do anything in the garden. He was, I suspect, deliberately incompetent. It was not long before I took over as well as these chores the financial running of the house, the paying of bills that previously had got lost in amongst the flutter of James's papers, and the general organization of all the things that need organizing with a large family. Longman's were very good to him and seeing that he was about to publish his second novel, agreed to let him have two days off a week in order to write. Longman's further indicated their faith in James in agreeing to publish his subsequent novels. The arrangement worked happily and well.

James was then offered his first film script to do, which was a Ralph Dearden production of an original screenplay of James's called *Violent Playground*. It was decided that we could probably manage without the income that we had from Longman's and James left publishing and became a full-time writer. This meant that we were now able to take the children and live abroad, a way of life that James found very conducive to work. He did not speak well any of the languages of the countries that we visited, but he would enjoy working in a café or bar where there was plenty of atmosphere around him which he could absorb at the same time as not being interrupted by snatches of conversation. The transformation of James was at this time almost completed. He no longer cared much to be invited out to dinner, where he would complain he was expected to sing for his supper. If, mistakenly, I made some social engagement, he would complain of a tummy ache, sore throat, headache, anything rather than go out. He was happiest with a handful of his friends of many years' standing whom we saw frequently. They were people with whom he didn't necessarily discuss his work, but we had families in common, and he would suddenly throw himself into the game of entertaining the children, which he could do with wild and sometimes frightening abandon.

Probably nobody who did not know James really well would have suspected his hermit-like tendencies. On the outside he still seemed to many people a very extrovert character, but then they would probably not have known either how much he both loved and needed the sea or about his preoccupation with his own early death.

WHEN IN 1961 James arrived in California to work on a film script *(Mr Moses)*, which was the occasion of his first visit to America, he was in black despair. He hated the place. His first letter to me was filled with anguish and home-sickness and he described America as:

> Hell beyond all description, money, fast roads with bitches in big box cars (not one of which, may I add, have I even spoken to. I've never felt so sexless anywhere). The feeding is gross to a degree, there is less straight vulgarity than I'd anticipated, more kind of limbo-like Hampstead garden suburb life and everywhere is miles and miles to the next place. There's a very great 'relax kid' creed which surprises. I'm the most tensed up boy in the business. 'You don't have to give me 100% kid; you wanna swim Jim?' So good night doll, see you and thank you for the telegram which at the time nearly broke my heart.

For the first few weeks that he was there he fought tooth and nail against the American way of life, against the system, but eventually he found Malibu and the beach and was able to settle down to start writing the script which was the reason for his visit to the United States. When he was not struggling with the script for *Mr Moses* he was writing his own novel, which was then called *Magnificat*.

Diary

Magnificat

There's a mistake in the idea of the fluttering of bird's wings in the womb. This is not only too obvious, in the literary sense, it is clearly inaccurate. Hope is not such a cliché. Not so broad in its effects. Hope is more tentative than that. It touches very lightly. Take your finger. Touch thumb against finger as lightly as you can: lighter. That is life, that is hope. That is stronger and realer and much, much more permanent than the worlds and moons that burst apart. Touch again. Without that no wave could begin. Because of that, somewhere a sea shall always move. And it is that which makes our life everlasting. That is why my soul doth magnify ... no ... (Then the breaking technique.)

I start with Hope. I do not mean this play, I mean my life. I mean as a child, and my sister too. I was terrified of my father, I was ambitious, as a child, pressed by my parents. I now believe, far too hard, and yet right underneath, lies now as has always lain, real hope. The term 'manic depressive' seems to me uselessly inadequate. Anybody who hopes must be disillusioned, only to hope again. This is what my life's about. But throughout it, even now as I gradually cut myself out from the world – purposely here, in California purposely I'm rude, purposely I tease, because I tease only myself, saying 'How I'd adore to give into life again', but always not quite letting myself because if I'm worth anything it is as a reflection, a crazy sort of barometer, a magnified barometer of ordinary feelings ... But always, always, I love it again, and this, nothing else, seems to me now what I'm here to say. I'm scared that's to say nothing, and I'm therefore a writer without value. But I know enough to know I'm actually harmful if I lie. I therefore can't explain, can't communicate, only political issues seem to me trivial. The real truth is that even in Germany as a Jew, I believe I would have found it possible to Hope. Is this what Christ did? Am I, just, in the end the last of the renaissance? another lost name in the only movement that really 'improves' us. Dare I suggest I'm that? It's my wildest dream. If I'm that, then I belong. Then I'm prepared to lose my name, to die.

To believe that some child, generations later, will feel the edge, that taste I've felt, and rise up, curly haired and say 'Yes' to life again.

At 11, I remember I lost all my hair. Before that like my DAVIE, and it kills one how much I love him, I was straight haired, straight forward and fair. After, it grew dark and curly, and with it I think grew a kind of aggressive hope. I'd been left out for 9 months. I was no longer a conformer, I was someone who understood conformity. It occurs to me suddenly that this may well be what they made me, so passionately to want to record, which is to say to write, which is to say to worship.

I shall be ashamed of this notebook. But don't let me tear it up. Its very childishness must have a value. If I studied before I wrote it, it would be as false as Willie Maugham's.

Changing for dinner, God knows why, after all the serious stuff today – after yesterday, last night and all that, I was cheered up by the thought that one might do something quite original in a comedy line on the hypochondriac (a Molière hypocrite). It could be started by (fantastic but true) the dentist curing fibrositis by changing a stopping on one's teeth ('off balance'). (A true story that.)

And suddenly rushing across the room he took her hand in his, one in each of his own, and crying he said, I promise I am not a destroyer. I didn't set out to be that.

23 June '61

A bird flew into my room, last night, midsummer's night, and it let me catch it and take it to the window. And I felt really marvellous suddenly when it flew away.

Then, with the family flying soon, I began to wonder if this was a good omen or a bad, frowning like my mother.

At last I decided to make it the most marvellous sign: you are freeing yourself. And that is to say you will work well.

For the last few days, I've been stuck and concentrating really very badly which is unusual for me. I seem to be blocked by too many ideas, and they're of such pressing kinds that I can't make myself think of *Mister Moses* for which I'm duly being paid my 50 or 60,000 dollars. Sometimes I wonder if it's the money that puts me off: or if it's just because it's somebody else's novel. I don't think either of these things are true. The terrible turbulences of the last two weeks have left me, psychologically in a most exhausted state. Yesterday for no reason at all (and I don't believe that!) I fell asleep three or four times during the day. When I awoke I struggled quickly to my feet guilty that I should have caught myself still asleep, after lunch at nearly five. I had gone to bed at two, I think and the night before I slept seven hours. As I say I jumped guiltily to my feet and because the house has big sliding glass windows, I mistook one, thinking it were open and crashed against it, and fell down. Then I couldn't get up again for a while.

I swam and ran about the beach for a while, about midday yesterday. Then in the evening pulled myself together and went to Frank Ross's* house, where unfortunately I just missed meeting Clifford Odets. We had a nice dinner and Chateau Lafite to drink that was superb. After that we watched *The African Queen*, which has much in common with *Mister Moses*, African adventure with comedy. There's nothing to be ashamed of in that.

At 12:30 we split up, but I was restless and went to one

* The producer of *Mr Moses*

or two nightclubs, saw a lot of big girls dancing and stripping, one of whom had my attention for about a minute. But they're remarkably anti-sexual. Or is it that one's always half exhausted when one falls into such a place.

At about half past three I prevented myself from writing one or other of the two works pressuring on my mind – not to mention the two that need work; all apart from dear *Mister Moses*.

But this morning that bird banging on to the very same pane of glass that I was and then suddenly it was taken gently in my hands and set free – this can take on silly proportions, I know. But I'm shifting now, noticeably, from the agnostic view. I cannot help myself coming round to God again and I feel happier, already, at the thought. This may be *Magnificat* and that, I'm not sure. It started and should remain primarily a piece about birth and hope, but suppose I set it in America then the *sensibility* argument is bound to creep in ...

From Mauriac (Oh master, master!) describing, in fact, a French bailiff, but substitute American business man: – or even the nation.

I find that in order to believe in the things I want to believe in, namely the soul, namely delicacy of feeling, namely aspiration, namely art, that these become quite useless and bogus unless achieved in the name of Gods that guide us. Suddenly one is sure that atheistic art is a contradiction in terms, like one of those blazing shafts of light, I suddenly feel absolutely certain of this and of course it swings one's whole terms of criticism topsy turvy. But never, and one must be grateful to America for this, never have I felt quite so sure that I've got something to say, until now. And however I refine it and dress it up and present it, this is its first form.

'Come to America and feel utterly starved. Realize that there is truth in art and sensibility. Examine that sensibility and you'll find some extremely delicate, almost invisible connection between the person concerned, and his or her own maker.'

So America, by a hundred contradictions, edges me again to all the questions of faith.

Oddly enough the same values i.e.: same lack of values, the same complacency which drove me out of Scotland, which I suppose, drove one to write in the first place, here faces me again. And this is my business. I'm certain of it: Not to fight for Renaissance knowledge – I'm an ignorant person – but for renaissance sensibility, for the Christ of Goya's which remains always my inspiration …

Oh God. As soon as the pen hits the paper it comes flooding up again. Yet I mustn't do this, or I'll never get *Mister Moses* done, and *Mister Moses* is by definition, by medium, almost, a story without all those points of sensibility – of the spirit, of the soul, of sacrifice, of what we feel at our most tense and most hopeful – why else do we write of the young? These things must have a value. This isn't romanticism. It's a question of struggling now and fast against a terrible piece of evolution that's going on: we're going to lose a whole set of senses unless we fight like mad for them now. These are the same senses which people like Cyril Connolly and Richard Hilary fought for: some with their lives.

My own position here is a nightmare. But surely I'm right to spend some time, under pressure now on this theme so that I can relax enough to concentrate on *Mister Moses*. Every time I think of him other thoughts intrude. I just can't help that.

Now as I write, and pace about, and feel about a thousand

times better, already, as if I never need sleep again, the mists begin to clear.

The novel, the viewpoint, all these which I was fumbling with in London, not knowing what I was saying become crystal clear. And for once this one can only be a novel, it being the viewpoint that is utterly important.

Much as I'm taken by the Mauriac method this technique has led me astray too often. It's anti-story pull and I think I'll brace myself and come round clean, to 1. As Jocelyn [Baines]* says, there's only one rule: choose the technique least likely to obstruct you in making your points.

Recollection of adolescent homosexuality poignant: of adolescent masturbation, a much more frequent occurrence, almost nil. Why? Because one has to do with sensibility, the other not.

I'm aware all the time that I'm using the wrong word in sensibility.

An actress, the other day, describing a situation which is I believe akin to her own, said that some girls who are afraid of sex are prepared to put up with the most terrible men: jealous, blackmailing, parasites, semiqueers, all sorts because the presence of this sort of man defends them from other men. They are frightened of sex. Ha! ha! we say wade in with the spades and bludgeons which Freud has left behind. But we may forget that in making her a 'well-balanced' person, we may be strangling something else. Is the memory, after all, such a waste? Is chastity a social virtue; is that all? Of purity of the puritans to the purity of the young. One's a denial, the other's a lark.

A couple of nice portentous notes after an afternoon, and a happy one beachcombing. I saw a seal, by the way,

* A colleague of James's at Longman's

basking, but didn't talk to him because he too obviously had big things on his mind.

11 July '61

First good thought for days!

Inclined, as before to write of a boyhood in Scotland? Yet feel not valuable but not contemporary – what a different world ... But surely if (Freud again) our behaviour is conditioned by our childhood then our destinies are to some extent controlled by the childhoods of men in control now. Besides, on a deeper level, it is our childhood we remember with clarity and pleasure and it is our comfort to know that at the end of life, whether for a second or for an eternity is as unimportant as it is in my stories, we shall again return to that land where it's always country, and always June.

Once James had come to terms with the appalling suggestion that he was supposed to work daily in the office of the film company from nine to five, he started to look for a place so that I could bring the children over to the States. He found a house perched on a cliff overlooking the sea. The beach was deserted. Seals and pelicans were to be seen if you were quiet and the house itself was delightfully remote and very fine for our purposes. I had not been to the United States before and the children and I were dazzled by the huge open car that James brought to meet us at the airport and the music from the car radio as we drove down the freeway.

12 July '61

Often, as I've probably said already, somewhere along the

line, I walk along the shore and I'm happiest then ... Tonight was particularly sweet perhaps because it was cloudy and the waves a little frightening and one could have been in Brittany (where I haven't been since I was 2!). And when I came back to where I had left my shoes a tiny brown, slim figure in a blue dress ran all the way along towards me as if there were bad news. And I waved and smiled and did something funny as she approached, to test. Then she smiled. There was not bad news, but a long story of Emma having got frightened by the T.V. which she had stayed to watch when Susan and all the others drove off to the shops. She went to the Briggs' (our neighbours) house, but found only the big dog – (*exactly* like Lassie) so she came down where she had promised not to go, namely the shore, down the steps where the snakes are. ('Davie's seen 2 snakes: we've only seen one. They're perfectly all right, you know; but I'm scared stiff. I get startled by snakes.') On the beach she had found my red shoes which I had discarded, followed my track. But I went a long walk and she turned back, 'feeling very *lonely*, very lonely indeed' and shouted for me, but I was not there. Then just as she determined to go back through the snake-land again she saw the tiny figure in the distance and hoped it was me. All this told me, backside foremost, and we came up and sat down and drank Coca-Cola, me with bourbon in it. We listened to the 'funny' record (Borge on 'Punctuation') then Schubert. Trout. ('You bought that in *France*, I know you did ... and once a long time ago I saw Mummy and you having a joke in the bath. A long time ago. You were!') Then the others came back yelling that they had had presents because they *went*, they didn't stay at home. But the cloud was not too heavy and I thought 'Fine' because the dialogue is of value, always: it is the best present. So a quick kiss, smack, good-night, and that's that. One could hardly say, 'As a matter of fact, little one, my heart has nearly broken in two.'

So many, many emotions and ideas still crowd in: this book gets about 10% I suppose, not more, that I know all the forms I suggest to myself could never contain them, if I lived to be a hundred. I am sure I'd be right to try poetry now. The rheumatics in my arms, tiny twinges, tell me this is a farce. I'm too late. Then I look at myself and know this can't really be true. I'm not an adult. I don't suppose anybody is. I play the adult: only that. Which is to say, that poetry must still be possible. I'm confident the language will follow – As I walk I know the sort of poetry, I know where it stems from ... I'm always frightened by the classical educations of the snob poets, but after all one has one's own education, one's own background. Why can't I call the loved one, instead of Chloe, or Deirdre or Persephone with all that myth from Odysseus to the others that I can never remember, why go there, when so easily I can choose a name from myth I'm much more at home with and I shall call her Mary Morrison.

Something, something ends in 'shore,
Nothing else: nothing more.'

Intimately connected with that patch of ground at the angle of the triangle at Shepherd's Bush. And browns and marine blue. A contradiction lies with eyes and the sea: at the gloomy moments the sea darkens, reflects the clouds. The eyes can do the opposite. Be filled with light like sea on a sunny day: on a coral shore.

It seems to me just possible that one of the male/female enigmas is that every man has two images, two views – the possible and the unapproachable ... Often, because the dichotomy is unbearable, he slips between the two, mocking himself for a second, abusing the first, hence brothels – hence jazz, etc. Hence escape into a lower form of sensibility. There's a very, very bitter, *Boule de Suif* plot lurking around here when we find that this is also true for women: that the whole thing is a circle of deception. That we are all as weak as one another. Four people sit upon a cloudy memory: the truth is laid bare. That's all ...

In 1962 he wrote in his diary:

I made a mistake of looking through this book. I suppose it's for the dustbin; adolescent wailings at 33 don't read well. But maybe that's how we come to stories. Sometimes wonder if I'm getting 'out of touch' but I doubt it; not with four children and Susan, whom I love; the only one in the end.

In 1962 we decided to take the children and go to Kashmir. James had made enough money writing scripts in America to give us six months off and we had no difficulty in deciding that we wanted to travel eastwards. The children were perhaps a little young to take with us but at the same time too young to leave at home, and so we took their governess as well. We lived on a houseboat in the middle of a lake and every day we could go and swim or the children could take pony treks or we could go fishing in the mountains in the snow-grey streams where the trout were abundant. James found it easy to work in these conditions and we would not readily have come home had not David, our youngest child, fallen ill that same year with suspected meningitis.

James waited in England long enough to ensure that little David would be all right. He then set off for Canada, where he met Anne. After his return in 1963, it was not long before he told me about what had happened there. Later that year, we both met David. This briefly, then, is the story of our lives up until the time of that dinner party in Highgate.

ALL THESE THOUGHTS and many others went through my head that afternoon after I walked out of the bedroom in Zell-am-See, leaving David and James alone. I went upstairs and locked myself into an attic, took a few pills and slept away the afternoon. After it was dark, Denys and James came together to the door and after much persuasion I opened it. It was evident that David had gone. James was disarmingly attentive. He had gone out with Denys to the town and they had bought a little gramophone and a few records to entertain me. They had also prepared an elaborate dinner, little pieces of smoked fish and pâtés. I was aware that James was anxiously watching my face for any sign that would imply that I had forgiven him for what he had done, to release him from his guilt. But I was unable to respond. I wanted to thank them for their trouble because I was used to saying thank you but I even felt too numb to do that. My whole world was upside down and there was James cracking jokes and being the life and soul of the party. For two or three days we never mentioned David and James did, I am sure, try terribly hard to please me. But I was too shocked by what had happened. I thought it was easy enough that he could be so cheerful since he was clearly the winner.

And all this time I continued steadily organizing the children, their meals, the house, the shopping, the laundry and James's shirts. I put my make-up on, very carefully, every day and washed my hair, and to the outside observer we would have seeemed to be a normal, happy family.

Some Gorgeous Accident

'Susie, you're damned right. We'll get out of it all. Get a shirt and a shave. Cash some kind of cheque. Get right out. No other explanations. We don't need that.'

No reply.

'Susie, you're the only one.'

'Susie, he really let you down.'

Still none.

'Susie, you look so pale. You're all right. Here's a hanky. That scratch. That's a nasty bruise. Link's got a hanky, even if no shirt. Maybe he put that on a horse. Did you get any sleep, Susie? Or don't I ask that?'

Susie's jaws locked.

My coldness and depression deepened and with my silence James became frustrated and then angry. We started to quarrel again so that then the children inevitably became aware of what was going on. Their ghost-like faces followed us, bewildered and unhappy. I felt that the only thing that I could do would be to return with them to England, leaving James in Austria, which he said then was what he wanted. I was to take the children home by train.

While I was packing for our departure, the telephone rang. The children had been skiing with their governess and she called me from the town. Little David had had an accident. I did not know any of the details but I went through to James and said that we had to go down to the hospital at once. What had happened was that David had skied ahead of the others and coming off the slope had failed to stop at the road and had tumbled head-first into a moving army truck. He had hurt his head. By the time Guy and the governess had reached the spot, David had gone, but an excited crowd pointed to the blood in the snow and said that he had been taken to the *Krankenhaus*. Neither of them was sure what this meant. It sounded such a terrible word, but they were given a lift to the hospital, where I found Guy trembling in the doorway. My German lessons had failed to equip me with the correct vocabulary for dealing with hospitals and it was with some difficulty that we finally made our way into the small operating room where David was being held, fighting and inconsolable, on the lap of a nun. They were putting the final stitches into his shaved head. I believed it to be my fault and a divine retribution for my conduct. I could not look at James, I could not speak. I picked up David and tried to calm him. The nuns insisted that he should stay in the hospital for the night, but at least we were able to take him home the next day.

I could not explain to James how I felt, that it was my fault, that I was responsible. So to make up for my silence he anticked around David, making funny faces and playing games and providing David with the sort of entertainment that only James was capable of, when he was in the mood. Since the children and I were leaving the villa we decided to give the governess a holiday so that she could enjoy some skiing on her own before returning home. It was a sorry little party, therefore, that arrived at the station, David with his big bandage and Guy trailing behind, still hoping that he might be able to stay, aware I suppose that something was dreadfully wrong and why wasn't Daddy coming with us? Up until the last minute I think James hoped that he could persuade us to remain there. He drained my confidence by insinuating that I could not manage the journey with the children by myself, but I was determined to go and could not wait to get away from the awful doom of that villa. James stood forlornly on the station, waving us goodbye, and the boys did not know why I was crying. I felt quite desperate for James. I ached with compassion for his situation and minded dreadfully that he would be lonely, that he wouldn't be able to look after himself properly, that he would smash up his car, fall into a big hole on the mountainside, get too drunk or be hopelessly unhappy. But at the same time living with James had become an impossibility. For the last few weeks he had watched me all the time and never let me out of his sight, I suppose so that I should neither make a telephone call to nor receive one from David, or receive from or write him a letter. The combination of the white walls of snow built up around the house and James's ever-constant attention were too claustrophobic and there was nothing to do but to go. I was not even sure whether I should see him again.

Some Gorgeous Accident

Then suddenly she returned to defending Fiddes. 'He's not so gutless, you know. The only thing wrong with him is that he's your faithful friend.'

Link tried to giggle.

'Susie, he doesn't even claim to be brave himself.'

'He's not so gutless,' she said again.

Once I arrived in England James wrote to me:

Letter to Susan

Zell-am-See
Monday 1st March 1964

Darling,

Should I write to you? No? Yes, yes, I should. I should never stop writing to you, even if it's a question of shouting to the deaf. I look forward to your next letter in Menton and I think I'll set out tomorrow or the next day. Clouds cover the sky at last and I had a bad skid today.

Words are so suspect, as we know. Much as I've tried them before the horrid little Scot locked up inside has betrayed my best intentions. But he will never win. It isn't James and Jim, by the by, that's all bluff. It's much deeper than that. It's life and death my darling. That is what I'm fighting, and that's why you must listen. 'Comedy' is a nice idea: was a good way to part: *Shoreditch*★ film is a nice idea too, and means nothing, nothing to me now.

My concern is how we meet again. That's all. And you must now listen for this, I swear, is the last staircase from Watford† and you mustn't now take the easy way. Nothing that has been said, however hurtful, seems to me without some basis. Yet I haven't got through to you at all. And unless I can get through to you, and make you see that you still have a whole developing life with me, then I know I've completely failed as a man. That does not mean as a writer, though I am also sure that it would diminish me as a writer. More than David I have connected living and writing which is why I'm writing more profoundly *at the moment*.

The best moment in the bloody exchanges that have taken place was when David came back – never mind the subsequent circumstances: it seemed impossible for me to let you go without being driven; I promise, promise, no bluff, so mad, that for the first moments in my life I no longer loved you. And that meant fear: fear: fear. But had I got across to you my situation, I would have stood it, as I can stand it now, away from you. Provided you read. Provided you try, try to get beyond that silent obstinacy which is not altogether strength.

This is no comedy, darling. Be fair to all. We seem to have become toys of the gods. And I will not tolerate an out-come in which all three are finally separated. If anyone is going to be separated it is me, I swear, not because I am the

★ *The Bells of Shoreditch*, a novel by James published in 1964
† Where I was born and lived until the war

strongest (we are all hopelessly weak in different ways), but because I have known more life than either of you and can therefore preserve myself, in the final instance, with less dignity perhaps, but more gaiety.

How shall we meet again? Only in one possible way. That you have opened your heart again to the idea that you are on a journey that is by no means finished, with me. You *could* have been with David, of course. But that is not the *fact*. I could have been with Anne but I recognize that was not the *fact*. I said in anger, 'I want you in my grave.' That's only half the truth. Your torn womb, torn having my children, is my grave. There is no other eternal comfort for me. This does not mean that you are my mother. Nothing clearer has come out of this than that David and I are whole men. You're woman, and we've all pushed ourselves to the edge of civilization, the case being special only in that we all love each other. Nor does it mean that you have silently to support me in dying and death as you have done in the past. I may have no torn womb, but I have battered shoulders and heart for you and I refuse now and always – because I recognize the *fact* – to keep them for anyone else.

'This', you reply, 'is what I said.' But that's a bad reply, because it's cheap on David, and that's where I'm beggared every time. 'You are a 34-year-old woman leading that young man by the nose' comes back to me, with horror and of course it was calculated to say what any of my easy comforters can and do say: what about that operation? ... I hope we're all better than that, though we cannot deny, again, the *fact* that while my life is over without you because my heart is worn out, so yours is without me, because your womb is no better and no worse than my heart. While you can hurt me by saying 'I could begin again with David who has never known our kind of happiness' I could equally hurt you by saying 'I can begin again with Anne or A or B or C, who wants my children'. And such a conflict is a belief of all we have together tried to become; of all my hectic fight against that horrid little Scot. We are both then diminished. David then loses two loves because both have clay feet, and are only an extravagant example of ordinary middle age.

I think our problem is easier than David's though I'm in no position to be confident. I'm trying to be true. What David offers you can be equated with what Anne offered me; the fallacy is that we cannot find within ourselves the satisfaction of those needs. We have failed to. But if I understand your love for David – and I never for one second underestimated it in spite of all the blinds and lies – then isn't it possible such support lies also, somewhere, still to be found for you …

Life has not been terrible. I deny that. In truth it was terrible once only for half an hour leading to Zell-am-See station when I wished to destroy you. Never, otherwise (to the detriment of others), has the image of what started half orphaned in S. Africa and is now already a woman beyond comparison in all my circles – never has love for that whole person subsided. And yet she is not whole. She is not there. Her elusiveness, her checks, her brakes, her suppression and repressions have driven me wild.

I would not expect a life to be completed in a moment. And there are all the twists in my personality and in my failure in love also to be cured. But if you come back, my darling, don't think it will be a life of hankering and martyrdom.

There is a fulfilling life with me still, or no life at all. I love you not only for what you have been, for what you are but for what you are yet to be. You are no chattel. I have never been complacent about you.

How you deal with David, therefore, I cannot prompt or know. That is an area of secrecy which I not only respect, but strangely love. How David and I deal with each other's love seems very clear, and unfailing, whatever. But I implore you now not to confuse your intentions and cheat; not that you would do. And I implore you to listen – to talk as much as you like with David of this letter or any other – but still to listen to me, and to believe in my love; not to say all passion, no love – how that hurt, David's words – not true. And to ride facts. To know where we are on such a turbulent, but such a rare journey. Oh, darling, I love you so – I must go out to tea with the Countess Esterhazy. (true!)

Love, James

When I arrived in London I was sad and lonely and rather imagined that James might be the same. I thought of him in the gaunt house up the white mountain, but perversely he would telephone me and say how much he was enjoying himself. During the time that we were in Zell-am-See we had rarely spoken to any of the people who lived there or who went there for their holidays, so it was with some surprise that I learnt that James had launched himself on the social scene. He made good friends with some Austrian aristocrats and told me that he had been skiing with them and to parties. This was very out of character because he rarely wished to become involved with new people, and yet it seemed to me that now he was having rather a good time. Only later, when I read his diary, I realized that underneath the joviality he was terribly lonely, turning for help and comfort wherever he could. I know he tried to find Anne in a desperate attempt to fill my place, but I do not know if she ever replied to him. Glamorous as the life was with his new-found friends, sooner or later it had to end, when the snow went and the tenancy of the house expired; and so James decided to travel first to Italy and then on to Germany. It was the spring of 1964.

Before leaving Austria he wrote to all his friends. Most of the letters he never posted. It was a habit. I found the letters still in his notebook. Mick Mulligan of jazzband fame never received his letter and so never met him at Nice.

Austria   Kennaway – cuckolded

Dear Mick,
Thank you for the warning (unheeded). Yes, Susie's fucked off with the 'innocent'. And I don't know whether I'm laughing or crying. It may not all work out but in the meantime I'm writing to keep myself from wanking. I'm in Austria but going down to Nice/Menton in a couple of days. If you could get off for 7 days, it wouldn't cost you any more than your return fare to come down to Nice and kick me up the arse or tear glands. I'll get a gaff for a week or two. If you thought 'okay' then cable Poste Restante Menton. Otherwise, see you, love – miss you.

James

P.S. Gaff will be near Hotel Eden, Mortola, Ventimiglia, Italy. But post over border to Menton.

Having left Italy, he went to Munich, not knowing the town at all or anybody there. With his usual instinct he found his way to a bar and settled down. It was called the Petit Paris. The young manager, Rolf, was a student who had abandoned his psychiatric studies. He and his girlfriend Renata soon became involved in James's problems and took him under their wing. He found a room in the Hofbrauhaus and every day met his new friends. On the telephone, late at night, he would talk to me in London about the wonderful time he was having. Here, too, it was only the subsequent reading of the diaries that made me realize that at the same time as he was leaping from bed to bed, he was nevertheless in a crazy downward spiral of depression.

Rolf I did meet later. Renata, Jacqueline, Sylvie: they are just names to me. James, inevitably, brushed the tip of the iceberg in telling me about the lovely, black, sophisticated Jacqueline, who even came to England to see him. He asked me to write a cheque for her. That was in 1967, I think.

Diary

Munich now – March '65

What one really should say to Susan with that agitated drive of hers towards David is simply '5 out of ten for wrong century'.

Perhaps people keep saying the Germans are foul simply because they're more people than anyone else. More real.

That cramped feel at night, with someone, when two fucks have gone and at last one says, meaning it seriously, goodnight. That awful cramp, first of the soul, second literally of the body. Why doesn't one part? In marriage one does, then when marriage is done one asks why didn't I sleep cramped all the time, because the cramp, the discomfort, seem to be the stuff of love, some kind of mutual yawning agony. Last night, E. talked so restlessly in her sleep, perhaps about the baby lost, perhaps about cramp.

Such a sweet-breathed cow, exactly that. Peasant ... The language was German so I couldn't twig what she said. But in Italian she only said she was sorry, she dreamed. Then we heard the maid outside (at 7 a.m., I suppose) getting sacked by the housekeeper for 'turning keys', thieving or prostitution? Thieving I guess. Then cramped, we looked towards love again and somehow performed the pain, the yawn, the restlessness to the pleasure and the point. Then it was time for a foam bath, and to smuggle her out, saving me money. 'Goodbye' and 'Grazie'. That's all.

It's quite certain to me now that an Author is not a character worth talking about, worth analysing because the contradiction is one too many: he is the actor to end all actors because he is driven by the people within, that vast family of cousins ... He's a kind of rickety candelabra (there was just such a one in the Haus am Berg) in which all the lights don't work all the time. They come off and go on again due to outside circumstances. The man in the street, the girl in the bed, whatever sets a light. She or he resembles closely enough the character already hidden in the head for there to be illumination bright enough to demand attention: to be written about or *acted out* sometimes, so close do fiction and fact become.

And it occurs to me that may be true. Then why so little written? What was the block?

The block wasn't Susan so much as the relationship with Susan, I guess. As this last crisis developed I gradually began to suspect that Susan's spiritual withdrawal was knocking me altogether too hard, turning me for that half hour leading to Zell-am-See station quite literally mad:

possessed. Then broken down, screaming, with Denys picking up my bowels where they lay all over the place. I thought that the storm centre was not the triangle at all and daily this becomes more clear. The real node of the storm was the struggle to admit to myself that I was 'nasty' enough to drop her like a hot potato.

This morning, though I was very tired, I began to see the possibility of a glorious freedom. Began to think with love again. I remembered once I said Germany was my spiritual home; for twenty years I've denied that strenuously, afraid perhaps of its truth. I don't know. But I like these people: the life in the Hofbrauhaus and so forth is so classless and scruffy and real and there's a nice sense of the possibility of any old man shoving his elbow up an 'eighteen year old's' apple-cheeked arse.

The old man who takes the girls back from the Petit Paris, by the by, makes a pass at them, always. He must be 65 with a sailor's eye, and they deny that he sometimes succeeds. I think he does.

At the Petit Paris, the system, of course, is very clever. There is a kind of justice, if instead of 'teasing' you describe the property bought and sold as 'dream'. And there are dream buys, spending 100s of dollars again and again. They go back and back *until* – and there's the point, the subtlety. Until one of the girls fucks. Then they never go again. Because it isn't a dream house any more. Reality has leaked in. It's a pick-up joint, leading to a prosaic conclusion, probably in a motor car parked in the slush.

The weather is delightfully depressing: truly *Maclaren's History* with snow in the streets, drab overcoats, pasty faces. I look very brown and slim and fit in spite of the fact that I thought I would die this afternoon, die of some internal burning, exhausting cramp. But I haven't wept yet today, which is a record for a month. Perhaps my egoism, this artist 'thing' makes me at least safe. I'll go down for it. Die even. That's safer.

The next section, Chapter 6, is giving me inordinate trouble. And I've got scraps of paper that must be put together. I realize the 'gang' is the trouble and Maclaren himself seems to need new depth around this time. It's at that nice after breakfast stage. One knows very soon the cramps will produce the most terrific onslaught of shit.

Had one only kept a locked notebook one would never have sent all those telegrams and letters over the years: all sincere: none the truth. No wonder we like women. They are our sisters. Writers, I mean, by us.

About the children. Of course I want them to be about again, and I dream of having Jane with me alone for a while: and wonder if she'd be happy. I think it could save her from the 'unwanted' thing, partly Susan's fault. Mainly her position in the family. But I'm helped here by Sartre's *Mots* and my own father's death. Fathers should soon withdraw. I may well be able to work that with a lot less harm done than anybody else suspects. And even if there is harm done temporarily, yet if I write better now, I believe, believe yes I do, that my boys especially, but also let's hope the girls will in the end recognize that a man must do what he's worked to do; is maybe born to do. In other words if this is a necessary break to make me work, I don't think one should feel guilty about it. Nor should my children in their time. Dammit, my father removed himself in the most damnable way. The fellow died, work unfinished – hardly begun, restless as he was. You can't do a son much more harm than that: or could it be, you can't do him more good?

The hate-love thing, so obvious, makes one wonder really about marriage. This could be simple defensive material but I don't think it is. Possibly only Byron and Co. had the courage to do what we should all do. Admit that the altar breeds hate: not only the altar, the vow – even the kind of vow Anne and I took, and doubtless D. and Susan are at this moment taking in each other's balmy and cramped arms. Killing the future with an eternal vow.

How wonderfully close fiction and life have suddenly become. And all moving to reality. It seems a blessing suddenly, the whole thing (though I suspected it from the start) and I seem to be moved not to recollection in the lock-up Proustian sense, of which I've been so afraid, but to a different kind of related loneliness. The lights are going on and off in that candelabra much more frequently, and they blaze, blaze, blaze, each and every one. My real fear, what makes me really cry is that I may fail to grasp this hour which some authors may never even know. I fear I'll shamble back and lay my head where my life has been, to Susan's belly and pad. But I know I shall love her much more if I don't: even if I don't see her again. Death hovers a little – many, many dreams of Winston saying 'Go on, I should have painted'. Old man sitting up in bed trying to understand me, rather in the Edith Shaw manner, when she fell against me that day before she died. Death hovers about. I think it's only fear disguised.

Denys persisting in a dichotomy that's not quite the truth (James et Jim), said in fury, in one of ten crises, 'what's this private soldier with a soul?' or more or less. But is that so bad? Surely harsh reality with a sense of immortality is what European man has been and should be again?

Rolf who manages the Petit Paris is a psychiatric student, taking a suspect couple of years off making money. That apart we've already had some quite penetrating wrestling matches, one of the points I definitely made was to open up the dread of competition and of course it is out of our own mouths etc. Indeed we sometimes wonder if one's fascination for other people isn't almost a totally self-illuminating trip, but competition in the areas of my own meant crisis could possibly be of importance and therefore I must soon have a go at inspecting it. Thrown unwillingly into something which we both deny is competition, I because I lost both times, he because he won.

Reading Brecht which is good but so depressing spasmodically on Jung who seems so far to base a theory, a whole synthesis on no premise beyond 'over 20 years of clinical work have led me to believe'. Hofbrauhaus Sunday 16/17 March. The *Maclaren* Chapter 6 opening scenes at last seem to be off the ground.

Poverty and religion: I am going to get the clinical answer then try beyond, and always in the middle a little girl walks through, that damned bold woman, my unfaithful wife.

Jacqueline arrives in my life. A strange tea party mainly climatized by Renata/Rolf situation. Lots of Bach-mit-Sahne. Jacqueline? Well on the whole yes, I think so, though I wouldn't have in the first half hour and of me? No interest in the first instance as usual.
P.S. Not true, not true the lady says.

Mainly for Rolf

A red letter day: same day, as above, only an hour since the moment, a moment I truly believe to be one of the important in my life. The actual happening was untroubled, the truth, so long resisted falling softly like a snowflake: inevitable, ineluctable, unharmful. Rolf made a move which I have funked making for weeks, maybe months, probably years – a truth which I could have avoided again for years. For him it was simple enough: presumably any trained psychologist could have done the same – though I like to think not so gently. It is also the first time I've had any *real* direct faith in the possibilities of analysis. In fact it was simple interpretation of a dream. And the revelation is as simple as daylight.

Because it's so important to me I want to write it all down, off the cuff, like this. But it *could be* of importance to other writers (e.g.: one especially leaps to mind: not my favourite but BALZAC who might well have had the same kind of complication bugging him).

I can't here again go through the last crisis, but when one has played over the scenes in one's mind again and again several extremely hurtful things, and other oddities stand out. There's evidence of them both in my agonized letters and telegrams to Susan and letters to her including one of only 7 days ago in which I described her 'torn womb' as my only resting place, or words to that effect.

(a) The first is what's been called 'the yellow letter'. About a year ago, fearing I was losing Susan's love I wrote her a note on yellow paper assuring her not only of my love but on the fragility of my own life; my dependence upon her love. The letter frightened and horrified her, had the opposite effect upon her that I wished it to have. It was for me a kind of second vow that I would not go with Anne after this, the parting was in the air, the only question left being whether we'd meet again, ever.

(b) David's (I'd known him marginally before) appearance in my life had several effects, envy, love, the idea that I was after all an artist of integrity who could help, and a man to set others free, that I was growing older etc. Paris meeting in August included a political triangle situation with the director who wanted to get rid of me, which David firmly refused; even resented. Of me, he said, 'Well, some of us seem to find it very hard to grow up ... ' That stung, because in many ways I found this to be true: yet in others, I knew and know that it is not in the least true. I grew up at 12, so school reports record, soon after my father's death; becoming head boy, belt of honour cadet, youngest prefect, etc., etc. The remark saddened me. I hate that director. I hated David for not having defended me more strongly.

The crisis came. I found the letter from Susan to David. To begin with I was perfectly prepared to accept the situation knowing that I'd had a much fuller love-life and fucking life than they. Then the temperature rose and I was shouting to Susan that night, 'My father let me down, everybody who matters in my life lets me down; because I can put on a gayer front on things than a baby like David, does it mean I'm not as vulnerable?' I shouted, 'I want you in my grave.' I shouted, 'My babies, my babies, my children, what are you doing to them?' I cried, 'You, Susan at 9 were left orphaned in South Africa deserted by parents: this is the precise repeat of the pattern. It goes from generation to generation of bad faith. We never get better.'

Then fucked off to Italy.

(c) After a loving despairing telegram to which I received no instant loving reply, I tried to cut my losses and sent two extremely insulting ones quoting (1) 'Dentist's wife' from Graham Greene's *Complaisant Lover*, implying my hatred for this kind of love affair, for the sort of 'adult' passion as described in modern literature which I find peculiarly unfundamental. David's strong similarity to Greene, as writer, gave the insult an extra sting.

(2) The other words were 'So long, crum-bum' from the prostitute scene in *Catcher in the Rye*. Prostitutes having played a bigger part in my physical and mental life than most men would care to admit. (I have dared myself before now to admit them fairly freely and in the present *Maclaren's History* Annie, the prostitute, is drawn from life and is one of the most vivid.)

(d) On returning to the house in Zell-am-See, Susan's withdrawal of love led me to make a gesture which had first occurred to me on reading 'the' letter. I wrote to them both wishing them well, saying they must go off together and David arrived. All went well until they actually went off to the train. Then appeared the hating, violent person who arrived on the station shouting 'you are a 34-year-old woman leading this young man by the nose'. There followed the only complete breakdown my life will ever know; of yells and screams and people dragging me home.

(e) Susan did not go. But continued to withdraw her love saying 'that young man led me *back* by the nose' and I've seldom seen anyone undergo the cruelty of the frost under which I then lived. Only an hour or two before parting did we somehow put a comic face on it and say, 'Well, well, life: no doubt we'll get through.'

(f) Left to my own I got in with new people, one of whom noticed that in trying to prepare a new life for myself I divided very sharply the artist and the man, refusing to defend the behaviour of the man, being fairly ruthless and arrogant in the protection of the artist. I actually wrote down words in this notebook for them to describe my reasons for refusing 'control': 'Let me scream like a child if I write like a man: let me die if I write like a god.'

(g) In the misery of the following lonely days I knew that the experience resembled only one other when first I was left at boarding school and screamed with fear and self-pity for 3 days. That scene, as well as father's death (which was 25 years before 'the' letter, almost to the day) recurred often.

(h) I've had terrible dreams. Work has been bad for me, although not impossible. I remembered only one corner of a dream which I told today to Rolf. Briefly: a child – NOT mine, but Susan's, I assume by David – and I are in a dark room and the child is in great distress. I called for Susan and she treated the child firmly but heartlessly. I remonstrated saying, 'That's not my child, but Christ, you're a heartless woman.' She sighs: leaves the room.

(i) I must (out of order here) record here my youngest son (David's) accident, the day before Susan and I parted. He had a bad skiing accident, running into a car and splitting his head open. When the hospital rang, Susan and I were together, we went down there together. She did not once appeal to me for support in what looked like a very nasty crisis, but kept herself to herself, making me for the first time sure that complete separation was in the air.

(j) The interpretation of the dream so clear to the outsider was impossible for me then to see. Who is the distressed baby? But of course. Me.

(k) Throughout the long post mortems Susan and I had with each other, with a friend Denys, even with David on his short visit when he brought Susan back, 'Jim the Schitz' was invented and Susan in tears shouted, 'It isn't Jules et Jim, can't you see, it's James et Jim.'

Following with this other group there has been much playing on the 'Gemini' theme, it supposedly being a bad period for Geminis (which I am). The division in my personality has always been apparent, but it's nature, James et Jim, man and artist, wild boy and introvert etc., never, never clarified. Never until now. Now not *cleared*, but there's a glimpse in that dream.

The artist is the baby. The baby is the boy I have had to protect since those first days at school. My violent hatred of reviews and critics and the Paris director (he was a critic) and yet my ability to take failure, with considerable courage and buoyancy, give away that it's the baby I protect.

I'm not at all knowledgeable about clinical literature. But I'm *sure, sure, sure* other artists of awkward cut-off-your-nose-to-spite-your-face kind like myself have a baby within them to defend; and that baby is themself, but somewhere along the line the pain was unbearable and the character split, one part ruthless in defence, the other preserved in original innocence.

I cannot tell you – and this part is for Rolf to read – what a revelation this is to me. However many errors may be contained, there is a blaze of truth, a great shaft of illuminating light that for the first time gives me a possibility of not only rest (and David has always said, 'You never rest') but also of maturity.

It alters, of course, it alters my whole view of the present situation. It alters it at once. The despairing need for Susan (as expressed in the last letter to her) is under control. Whether, on the other hand, we could ever live together happily – whether this discovery could alter, so late, her view and now to me understandable fears of my love – I don't know. But I no longer feel the drastic need which was 'certain' in my mind that I either had her complete love again, or never saw her in my life again. My fears for my children (I panicked on my own daughter's first advent to boarding school) were terrible, but I was saying to myself, 'It happened to me, so I must accept that it can happen to them' and was prepared never to see them again.

There is one curious fact. David's love for me has been in my view (now) a curious sympathy for the vigilant defence (I've dreamt a great deal of Churchill, talking to me saying, 'Listen to nobody, defend to the end') of the baby. And I now believe that his sympathy is too strong to be without identification. I thoroughly believe that Susan has moved from A to A, not A to B.

I feel I should put this to them both. I want to do so, at once, of course I do, but won't until I've thought further and even if then. We believe that I have fought through – been dragged through to a kind of sanity which I thought I'd lost. I would rather Rolf went and saw her or them in the first instance – at my expense, needless to add. But I'm probably jumping too far.

The other possibilities are to live alone, or with Anne who first knew my violence because she refused always to recognize the baby, so becoming what I thought of as my only full adult love. She might have nothing to gain, might not now even agree to come. Again, now, this is a perfectly bearable thought where it wasn't before. I can see quite clearly the possibility of a new stage of my life on my own, and not in the hectic colours which I had painted it, before. What happens to the baby or the man: do they merge? Do they live (more likely) in mutual understanding? I can't see the answer to that. But what is wonderful is that someone has uncovered the baby, the shame, the *golden* and beautiful child, and it has not dissolved under scrutiny. I still can write, I'm quite sure. Previously (I see now) I had thought that the uncovering of that secret would ruin me as a writer. And in defence of that child I have been quite prepared to fail as a man. I have not even tried to be a man. Not except in sabre-toothed defence.

I am also aware, Rolf, that what is happening is now rather frightening and I reply upon your cautions. But I will try *not* to do so, too much.

I wonder if in all young marriages the man is born twice? Such a desperate thought for the young bride or young groom. But the truth?

Monday. Really now it begins to get fishy. Quite clearly the Petit Paris is splitting because I am there. Rolf is in a situation with Renata that has swiftly developed the crisis. All I have done is to try to be good and unaggressive and undestructive and here's another bomb about to go up. I feel it is because I enquire that I must in each place do something worse than this. I think I ask too much of people, something like that. Now truly I feel if I went into a church and kept my mouth tight shut the roof would fall in. Perhaps unfinished man does this. But the Hofbrauhaus is firm enough so after the exertions of last night let us put our attentions again to the world of Annie Seaton.*

The subsequent discussions led to a first step in analysis though it was later agreed to dig only so far, as I'm so determined to finish *Maclaren's History* by April 10th. But the main and most encouraging step was 'What's a baby?' and of course a baby is probably the strongest force on earth. While therefore my essay above is a movement of confusion requiring clarification at once, the signs look fair for sanity. This conclusion has been arrived at really over two days. Meanwhile there's been a splendid Boswellian comedy

* Character in *Maclaren's History*

108

raging with Jacqueline and Sylvie. After bringing Rolf's
Renata to the P.P. when he least expected it I promised to
go round to the Pussy Cat and see Jacqueline. But the flirtation I'd had with Sylvie suddenly developed, extremely
surprisingly into a definite invitation from her to sleep
with her that night. I was not in a mind here to say either
yes or no, but on the whole implied sometime and she
pressed for the next afternoon. Went off to Pussy Cat, continued with Jacqueline to Playboy and of course she dances
with a superb primitive edge, this being the African menace
I guess. Anyway we got along very well though I did not
think we'd sleep together. Rolf arrived, slightly pushed us
into the idea and at last we said we'd take his apartment and
he came to my much confused hotel (where he was woken
at 6 a.m. to move my car!).

I then spent one of the most remarkable nights of my life,
our approach to each other was so gentle and careful that by
morning we were in heaven, and exhausted, so then we
have breakfast, she goes off to find an apartment for us, I
go to have lunch with Sylvie and because her understanding
of the situation is so plain I feel obliged to take her secretly
upstairs to my room where the proprietor of the Hotel dis-
covers us and there's a scene, this saving me, I guess, as I
question if I had the energy left in me. However Sylvie is
now more than ever loving and refuses the cinema for a
country drive. In the woods, my friend, and because there's
snow about we take so long discovering the woods with
her hand on my knee that when at last we get there it goes
with a bang and we even attempt a second but the old horse
doesn't make a fifth request in 12 hours. Back we come in
time for me to change and go off to drive Jacqueline (a great
writing day, this).

But Jacqueline has suddenly assumed the face of love,

much resembles Anne in her approach. She suggests we go to the Cote d'Or now I've finished the book. Say 'give me 12 hours', meaning yes, yes wonderful, I find myself dangerously near love. I return to the Petit Paris where I hear with real pleasure Rolf's first chapter of *The Group* which he has started, insisting that it's my idea etc. and that the credit must be joint. I promise whatever happens to return to Munich and read the draft then, help him to work it. He's broken with Renata, looks happier, but worried by me, not that he knows all the story. Sylvie is of course all over me, very sweet but so sentimental and sad about it, asks me to go home with her in spite of the husband. I say I have to go to England.

Return to the Hotel, and dammit there's a telegram from Susan saying ring me, love. We have a consultation in which for once I'm honest and as usual she's careful. But David definitely won't break with his miserable outfit; so Susan's now in the place I was, of losing both. The conversation rambled. I said I'd ring again in the morning and now I'm awaiting the call. Meantime Jacqueline had rung and I've told her about Susan's telegram, not the call and Sylvie rang so I told her in tactful terms of necessary return to England, hoped to be able to say good-bye ... but I will return sometime, etc.

An interesting enough 24 hours, if only as interesting example of difference in love of German and French. The German by the by, is good too, very, but the whole quality – well it needs an essay.

The next stage with Jacqueline and Sylvie is almost unbelievable plotty farce. In searching for an apartment Jacqueline is in contact of course with Rolf (now broken from Renata) and because Sylvie is a helpful kind of girl Jacqueline and Sylvie meet and talk and get on well. They even talk of sharing an apartment.

A night of single sleep passes, disturbed only by bad news of Susan, who is sad when I'm frank on the 'phone and is also a little self-contradictory. 'Parted to have a quiet time', 'David won't leave his family anyway'. But I obviously shake her a little too much by being perfectly frank. Anyway, it's decided that we won't meet for a while, and I lie to her saying I'll pull out of here and go to France alone. It's a lie of fact, not of kind.

I feel if it's on offer I might as well take cunt with me, though I don't know if Jacqueline will come. She wants to stay in Munich. I say no, I'm going to France, come or don't and then she arranges to leave her night club bar job. To find a girl, she thinks, 'I'll ask Rolf'. Again Sylvie answers the 'phone. I've promised Sylvie to go into P.P. to say goodnight. Suddenly it dawns that a bomb is about to explode when Jacqueline says she's coming to talk to Sylvie at 2:00. So I tell Rolf, purely as maître de scène in this case, and he is of course a bit surprised on the Sylvie front and we've had this horrible male talk on German and France/ African women. (Both by the by, are wonderful at sex though in utterly different ways.)

My penchant for Anne leads me to the unsentimental and therefore quite definitely to Jacqueline but this shouldn't take away from Sylvie. She has what I once had on a train, that kind of pneumatic tightness of flesh and cunt, and a very good manner of losing herself. (It's a kind of dream Victorian fuck.) Anyway, I'm now scared enough as it's obvious that Jacqueline will eventually say, 'Why I want another girl for the bar is that I'm hopping it to France with James.'

Now Sylvie has talked of love in the most sensational and suicidal terms. Rolf fortunately brought me back to earth by saying that she's probably even taken money fucking and the idea that this is the first time she's been unfaithful to her husband is ridiculous. This greatly strengthens me as I'm scared of hurting her. In walks Jacqueline looking exactly like Eartha Kitt in white furry collar and white leather coat. There's a big rush around and we extract Jacqueline from the club before she has a chance to talk to Sylvie. Pretending throughout that Rolf and Jacqueline are the lovers. (Why he is loved, by the by, by all the girls at P.P. is explained quite differently by Sylvie and Jacqueline. I think Jacqueline's is the better explanation, but there's always a language bar with Sylvie.) Anyway I come back with Rolf and Jacqueline to Hotel.

They sit in the foyer and I ring Susan to say I'm extracting myself from all this shit. She's very dazed on the 'phone, and had a nasty black-out when driving the children, which sounds dangerously like psycho suicidal and makes me think that David really must have let her down. She wouldn't give details of any meeting, she sounds bad and cast a shadow of trouble over me, but then I realized that we were only getting back into the same cycle if I turned back at this stage. So I said I loved her which she wouldn't accept, in spite of the glowing truth, she then *implored* me to let her go off alone for a few days. I said stop *imploring*, okay, but assumed of course that this is the, or another, David meeting.

I must say Munich has had one result, I'm much calmer about all that. I realize that what I shouted previously need not have been shouted. It's true, Baby, maybe, but I've seen so much more than her and I guess, him. They're ill matched really; he's far too young for her. So I can only wait and insist on some indication of truth (though if I take Jacqueline to France, I won't even say. What's the point?) Will I take Jacqueline with me? Well, as I will, she's an hour late and I don't know. Frankly I may push off alone with relief. Yet she's very sweet and I do want to go on fucking her quite badly. I can't believe in the masturbating writing line at the moment. The opposite is true, I think. Psychic and sex energy together build up and there's enough for both paper and women and more, once the heart is high. Oddly they seem to charge each other ... but I'm talking quite vaguely. Enough, I must reorganize from Chapter 6 to the end of Act 1.

Well, well you can't say we live a dull life. At last at 1:45 I went to the Plaza beer-hall to eat (very good too) thinking, well I'll leave after lunch, on my own: slightly sad. Not much more, and in comes Jacqueline with Rolf and they say she can't come today there's a problem – not another man. Eventually Rolf goes off and I do a short guessing game the second or third shot being 'baby', and it's right. She wants to get an injection against pregnancy of 15 days from the last (?) night she slept with her fiancé. They've been searching for this doctor. So I'm not very alarmed by this, and she cries and says I'm great so I feel okay but have visions of carrying a sick coloured girl through France, semi-poisoned by illegal drugs. Never mind, I've said I'd take her whether she can fuck or not, and it looks as though we'll leave tomorrow morning not today ... Chapter 6 does seem to be having some troubles. But really we must now get back to it. (Renewal by the by, of Jacqueline and Sylvie risk, Oh Hell.)

The diary part by the by is extremely difficult here for the old reasons. Who's going to read this – Susan or Jacqueline? Anyway to hell, she's with me.

Wrongly maybe we spent the night in Munich waiting for the doctor when lo! in the morning it happened naturally. There is no fear of the baby and off we come to France staying near Nancy for a very good Routier's type evening. I don't work. We continue to Hotel de la Poste, Saint L'Abbaye and I have an appetite for work. She's late sometimes but she's being perfectly sweet and so grateful and loving. I don't know whether I am doing good or on one of my usual destruction acts but at least this time I'm on firm ground wife-wise, work-wise, it being understood:

(1) I'm going back to family April.
(2) I'm completing MS. by April.

Not posted

Munich, March 1965

Susan

We now reach the stage to be quite frank when nobody recognizes that I can write, so probably I can't and the one person I love and have loved can't recognize my love, so perhaps I'm no good at that either. My intention therefore is simply to continue to exist, to write, I guess, but without deceiving myself that anyone will take it seriously. I'll see you soon, with this rubbish complete in some form and hand over the house and money to you for the children. I'll be back about the 25th, and will ring from the coast. I'll be there, don't worry. And we'll eat well, whatever. The laundry is the real problem alone. You don't think I know what love is. I'm damn sure you don't. Great. Absurdity complete. I'm utterly in love with you. So we meet with a laugh, that's how we meet. I'm not even confused any more.

Yours faithfully,

J. Kennaway

The letter 2 pages back shows half my heart. Susan sounded bitter and despairing on a short 'phone call, wanting me back to send away I guess, and now she says David's irrelevant, it's all my fault and has to do with Munich activities. I couldn't get it across to her that she was simply finding a way out of her present dilemma, an excuse for sacking me, (a) because then she could negotiate David or (b) because she still loved him even if he's refused to leave his wife or (c) because she's hurrying the crisis, driving herself to the point where she has lost both men, and no longer needs to fear it. Dale* on the 'phone said he wished I'd come back and sort things out – there's a good deal to sort out. I don't know. I'm depressed by the book, a little at present, though it *shapes* well. Jacqueline has been absolutely marvellous, washing all the shirts etc., making herself scarce when I'm at work, looking ravishing every evening, and of course sex is wonderful. She's constantly saying, 'I know you're trying to make me fall in love with you. I know your game. And you're succeeding.' But it doesn't seem possible for me to move on, with the heart. I would if I could but I can't. Yet Susan enrages me now. Of course with Jacqueline, French and vital and independent, I often wonder about Anne. But always the conclusion is the same. Susan is the reality of my life. Without her, no life. I'm too worn now to start again. One of Susan's most annoying contradictions is the business of saying that David won't leave his wife and then saying, 'But we were meant just to be resting.' In other words, typically she moved fast enough but because it didn't work for her everything gets landed on me. Oh dear. Christ knows what David thinks he's been doing. To ask her to

* Dale Harris, Mieke's husband

marry him in Vienna some weeks back and now to withdraw looks windy to me. Maybe I was right in temper. She is leading him by the nose. In which case, poor love, no wonder she's now in the state she is. But I'm the other part here. I can't comfort her for the loss of paramour. I can't play *all* the parts.

A curious recurring thought that could be true is that I simply don't believe in marriage. How I hang to Sartre's *Mots* on Fatherhood, also to the development of Susan into a girl: i.e.: out of a wife. The disgust with permanent personal relations, particularly of a social order. Maybe David's spotted this and sees it to be true for him too. Good on him, if so. And let's hope Susan comes round.

The book is at about page 410, on chapter 10, after 10 days' effort. The *credulity* is the problem, but there are some good things there, and in chapter 10 there seems to be a sense of pay off. I am about to start the *Echoes in the Grove*, and perhaps it's a good thing that I haven't the early part of the book. The natural distortion of the scenes may be effective atmosphere.

Jacqueline of course has been with me all the time and she's been angelic. Except for a moment's quarrel in Dijon and a tearful night two days ago. She couldn't have been more perfect. I love her. I'm not in love with her. I question if I'll ever be in love again. There are very strong resemblances to Anne, though she's not so clever and of course much younger. Some surprises included the cleanliness and order – all my shirts washed and all that kind of thing. We've lived expensively because the hotel is too expensive, but not extravagantly. She says she's in love with me and the arrangement is that she'll wait until May 1st before any new life. I really think I've done good here and I hope there's no 11th hour backlash. Rolf and Renata arrived this morning for a holiday which may engender complications. But I must depart tomorrow and we'll see (famous last words). She's made me feel more man I think than anyone. I feel very much that I guide her on an easy rein and physically the passion has been extreme ... this may be circumstances, may be in her primitive side. It is frightening what I can do to her and how effortlessly we seem to have come together that way. She's funny about her body. Feels its beauty (and it's perfect) comes between her and love, I think 'my bode-ee'.

I'm still so confused as to my situation at home that I won't know what I feel about Jacqueline for a while. It occurs to me that I may need her considerably more than I realize just now.

To Susan

> Hotel de la Poste,
> Saint Seine L'Abbaye,
> Cote D'Or

> Monday 15th

Sweetheart,

I mustn't start writing letters, nor must I consider too deeply what you said on the 'phone lest p. 303 takes the four weeks that it took to finish p. 183. To lose confidence at this stage – and for some reason I *feel* you want me to, you are attacking my talent – would be too bad. Do you remember St Seine L'Abbaye – in a big dip in the Cote d'Or by these mossy trees that shone so clearly once in the evening for us, when nanny Jackie was with us and David in the carrycot? I walk a lot: write: eating's good but not as good at it should be.

Please stop whatever's going on in your head. Just stop it and stop listening to friends who know nothing about us (Christ, I wish I could send David to tell you this!) Four months ago Mick and David said 'What a couple!' I love you none the less, I blame you for nothing. While you say you love another, by any rules worth having this gives me licence to open up new fields of experience. In Munich for the first time in weeks I stopped looking up your backside, forlornly, and that's that. Why the hell you should think that such a perfectly understandable (and extremely funny) aberration, interval, what you will – should make me incapable of making you happy again I don't know or do, but hardly dare tell you. Please don't lay things at my door, saying, 'I can't love you because ...' if the real truth is that you can't love me because of David. And please don't try and take it out of me because things aren't yet right for you. I'm not going to sit around trying to persuade you that I'm the martyr or the patient type. I love you. I cannot tell you again without becoming tedious, how much. I need you. I cannot write without confidence. The confidence comes from love, or in emergency from pretence love. The only thing therefore that astonishes me is your surprise at my reaction. It is precisely the same as David's would have been, by the by: this I know. It would be the same with any man that you're likely to love. So stop it, please.

Great comedy I must say. But we *both* went back on that. It's impossible for us yet to see each other's point of view. But that's not to say we haven't got one. But please, darling, I have never yet lowered things to *blame*. In a situation of love as hot as this we may react childishly, impatiently, dishonestly. But no one of us can rightly be blamed. Spring's here, more or less.

I'll ring old Watson. Now for p. 304. It's so complicated now, this book, love, baby – James.

(As soon as I've finished this section which leads well into the second act, I'll move westwards.)

Don't we both by the way do the same strange things? Because you fear losing both, you drive yourself towards losing both, so that you're over the worst. Not necessary, love. I'm here.

To David (Not posted)

St Seine L'Abbaye

David:

One of the things you and Greene and everybody must do wrong, and certainly I did in the *Bells* is not to give people a full chance. In your book this is prevalent throughout. You introduce say 'You call me staff', and you therefore *cleverly* give us a vision, an impression of a man. But in so presenting him, I think you've probably committed a novelist's error. If a character is to be mentioned he is never to be written off. There can't be a full investigation of every character of course, but such a 'summing up' in a phrase or more is *false* unless it is accomplished with a question mark. He must say more than 'Call me staff' – he must add something, somehow which suggests ... 'You don't know me at all. You don't know how I've suffered or ... whatever'. But we mustn't write character *off*.

J.

Diary

Susan rang sadly only once and said amongst other things

119

that she'd never sleep with me again, she must know that I can't live with her and NOT, so presumably she's rushing her fences. I had the mad idea of ringing David ... But I don't know, that could go wrong. And I'd hate to ruin that as well. I simply have no idea of what's going to happen, though I think I should depart from my family now. The writing is not good but I'm old enough now to recognize original talent in myself. And though I'd be lonely – and I at once fear death in a way I never have before – I guess I've a duty to talent more than to the family. The hatred of one's friends is more easy to bear than the disappointment and sadness of one's relations. I wonder how little David had to do with this? Possibly his faith in my talent has been more relevant than his nosing after Sue. Oh dear, the waves still break. I'm beginning to get a little tired too, after all these pages and fucks. Two or three a day for 20 days takes it out of the old man now. I've dropped to a slow one strike long-hole really. But fun. I felt my heart pounding last night and I began to see my grave again.

While writing *Maclaren's History*, the book that won't be called *Lady Fear*, starting from the relationship between Macbeth and Lady Macbeth, it occurs to me that death has always been associated with the subject and I shiver. But I don't think I can avoid it. The whole story seems to form in my mind, in spite of myself. Maybe I'll live alone by the sea in Barfleur and do it. I think that's what I should do, but of course the *Bells* complication is now coming up.

James says that I rang sadly and said amongst other things that I would never sleep with him again. I do not really know how he expected me to react to his announcement that he was sleeping with a beautiful, exciting, sophisticated and loving black woman. He was obviously enjoying an aspect of sex that we had not reached together.

Then David had to go to Paris to work on a script. He asked me to join him. With James's blatant taunts much in my mind, I could not see why I should not snatch this chance to be with David again.

It was so gentle being with him, and we pretended for a few days and shut out those awful memories of James at Zell, but the innocence was gone and the memories could not indefinitely be pushed aside. We dreamed and planned and all the time I knew that David would not then leave his wife.

David said that he could not destroy James further and that our marriage was the finest thing and should not finally be smashed. We had to wake from our dream and face the reality of our families; though with the thought of James's letters and 'phone calls, I despaired.

So it was hello and goodbye, again and again. And I love you, darling, for ever.

Diary

23 March '63

And once I worried that my life was not full enough to enable me to write. Now, really, the diary makes more exciting reading than the story. After a last and longing night which ego dictates completes the *épanouissement*, in which for once I had to take care against birth, Jacqueline and I have parted. She woke me this morning, she slept while I worked, and we discussed the previous night spent drinking champagne with the local routiers, in the restaurant up the road, who fell for us and asked us to stay and stay and go on dancing (tonight) in Dijon. A mild man and a beauti-ful, I guess, empty-headed wife *(pas Italienne mais Dijonnaise)*.

We talked laughingly about Martinique and I seemed to manage for the first time to completely transmit myself at my most outrageous, in French. It all went well, and we lunched there with R. and R. this morning. (Perfect routier stuff – I sound like one of those damned *Sunday Times* men.) Then we came up the Seine, almost my favourite road, all 'inondée' flooded gushing over green fields. Jacqueline completely loving and depending; for once I was honest in saying I was NOT in love but loving, and when we came to part in Fontainebleau she was marvellous and brave. As usual we've run out of money. The hotel at St Seine was ridiculously pricey (we should have fed always at the Routier) and I borrowed 500 marks (150 francs) from R. to be paid back AT ONCE. He's been sacked from the Petit Paris and is going to settle at the St Sulpice Hotel, where D. and I stayed, and where Anne's friend Madeleine stays: small world. I told R. and Jacqueline to try and find Madeleine. Jacqueline is going home to her parents. I gave her 50 and 100 for her journey home. That's all she has in the world. I'm really a capitalist. So much, much happens ... Tracking towards Barfleur completely by mistake I fell on the obscure village with a church and bar where D. and I stopped after we'd slept in the Citroen, one Sunday afternoon. Here he told me some of his secrets, the love life etc. It was an astonishing surprise to arrive there – a village with a low chateau near Etampes.

Now I'm in Chateauneuf, surprised to find I called here for Routiers' lunch en route to Paris in August. I think and I'm in what doesn't seem to be too good a hotel with a maid with a frightful cold she was determined to give me. Sleeping alone will be frightening again and driving on these smooth roads I wondered if men had built them only so we could hurry over the face of the world. But I'm so much happier in France than anywhere else that I can't believe I'll live longer elsewhere.

Of course my thoughts turn to Susan, wishing and praying that she might manage to start again, but I'm not too sanguine. It seems so silly when it's her I love. I don't think I could begin again. Really I don't: not even with Anne. Yet I feel energetic and quickly I turn my mind away from home onto *Maclaren* now that Chapter 10 seems to be working out. This morning I had one of those marvellous, rare, rare leaps of the heart when I suddenly thought as I worked – 'It's original!' The plot stuff around Billy Pinero★ is still a sore and I've got awkward stuff ahead in Chapter 11. I mean to go to Barfleur, tomorrow – travel back finally.

I know I fear loneliness as much as anybody else. But I also fear compromise. I won't think about it or I start seeing too many alternatives. The Germans, Rolf says, are poor philosophers because they're *too* introspective. How we *play* with the plots of our own life ... Now eat. I was here, an age ago, in July.

Because I am thinking of Jacqueline in retreat like this, it's exactly like Anne. Her colour goes and I'm left with the eyes, the eyes. I wrote this morning in the new book, of confusions, of intentions and that's still the problem. I had a long talk with Rolf yesterday and for a moment this morning. He's coming on with *The Group* – says he understands D's point of view very well. Odd. Must I extend my ego to those people. Can't they just say, he believed in writing, in art. Not wholly, but he helped, he really did, maybe to build himself up, but he did get other men to write – oh, that would be epitaph enough.

On return I wrote in the new book this morning, but have determined that this one should close at Barfleur. I

★ Character in *Maclaren's History*

want to give it to somebody: not a woman. Denys maybe? David? Why? Not David, no. I think later it might be very valuable to me.

Chapter 10, by the by, already contains much of it.

But it's a good hotel! And why do I present myself here as in life, as such a shit? The truth is I'd *like* to see David now, tell him how lousily he writes etc. Actually one of the bad things that happen is that people keep telling me they don't like David's book. And I say, 'What about the characters?' and they say, 'Well, yes.' Yes – but of course ...

Denys, I think: DENYS. HIS BOOK. But don't burn it, please, not yet. I *could* be good. And D. too. Neither one yet.

I'm going to have a lonely brandy now. Have NOT yet, writing now because waitress got cold and am leaning over the table. Is cognac *really* –

Wipe out these fucking photographs. I don't want them. Why can't someone burn the bloody album in my head.

To Susan

Susan:
I'm terrible again: I'm afraid I can't manage England. I can't comfort you. I can't see the children. They're already destroyed I guess. The book's unpublishable but I must keep at it somehow. The withdrawal of your love was the end, end, end, fin. Now I don't want to see you any more. Get papers from Bank and I'll hand over the house and some shares but I must have some to live on. If you're too bad then the kids must go to Hazel or my Mother for a while. Poor little bastards. It comes in waves. Sometimes I'm quite okay and I've taken a swear I won't tear anything up

though I don't want to read it. I don't think I can manage *The Bells** but that's all uncertain anyway, and there seem to be hitches. If you have 14 years of heaven, I guess you must expect the rest hell.

To Susan

I'm afraid things are terribly bad again, and I can't comfort you. The book is a fiasco at the moment and while it's in this state it's absurd for me to come back. Really things come in waves now and I don't know where I am but I'm no good to you or the children like this or for a little while you must just write me off. Maybe forever I guess. I can't bear the thought of England now so I'll stop at Barfleur then Graham† can come across and take the rubbish when I've tied it up somehow. I'm going to start straight away on the next, for which I'll need my Father's book, also *Culloden* by Prebble (I also need the Mary Stuart events synopsis, but I guess I'd better write to Sandy‡ about that). The writing is terrible but the ideas are so good. I don't want to see you.

J.

Letter to Susan

Dijon
April 1965

Darling,
I think the 26th is a Friday and I shall probably arrive at the Manor House that day or the previous one, but you can always redirect me by Poste Restante Barfleur – or better

---

* *The Bells of Shoreditch*, screenplay of his novel
† James's literary agent
‡ Alexander Mackendrick, the film director

still come and join me there. It's easy taxi from Cherbourg sea or airport.

The book is in a terrible mess and if we could get a secretary to come to the Manor from the Monday 30th onwards, that would be good. If you have to go to Edinburgh to the girls on the Monday I'll run you up in the Citroen which will save money. Could see the headmistress.

Spring's here and I'm working madly but not altogether with success. The obsessive quality of the book is very hard to sustain when one is rushed like this. I'm only hoping I can do a lot when I see the type draft. Please could you collect from Curtis Brown the typescript that should have arrived from Vienna and bring it to the Manor or Barfleur if you come across (there's only one main pub, I think it's de la Poste). I'm still trying to get out of going to Hollywood as I don't feel it would help *Bells* or me.

There is only one way to save our family. It is to look forwards, not look back. J.F.K. and J. once reached a stage like this. And for about the same reasons.

love,
James

James's progress up France continued to be punctuated by dramatic telephone calls and contradictory letters. His mood swung from unrealistic optimism to searing insults and finally self-pity. I could not see how we could possibly live together again. We had been too far apart, so much had happened, too much had been said, too many secrets revealed. Having thought I had lost them both, I had come to appreciate my lonely life. I could not see the point in going through it all again; I could not climb out of the sea of misery without

James pushing me back into the waves with his outrageous anger and sorrow and I could no longer see why I should even try.

He finally arrived home exhausted. I do not know what he expected of me, perhaps a miracle, but I could not just pick up the threads of our life as if nothing had happened. He pranced around, as if just wagging his tail would make me laugh again, and when I did not respond, he fell into a deepening gloom. I could not wipe out the pictures in my own head, let alone help him obliterate his.

I began to wonder if I myself were going mad, when all the evidence pointed in his direction. Such was the power of James. He claimed to have found a psychiatrist who could help him, feigned funk at the last minute and asked if I would go instead, so as not to waste the appointment. I found that he'd arranged for me to have the treatment. In the shock that followed I also found a friend. I really needed someone who could tell me that I wasn't the callous, cold person that James told me I was.

Meanwhile James stalked round me like a beast after his prey, watching always for signs that could be interpreted to my disadvantage. I believed we had come to the very depths of the ocean.

It was evident that if we continued together in this fashion there could be no future for us. James took the boys and moved to the country; I stayed in London alone.

Diary

May 1965

There's a slight muddle here. I began, as I remember, in a hard-covered type notebook and now seem to be using this one.

First the earliest MS. of the novel is shocking. It's beautifully typed but it's a load of balls and I must stop Dostoevskidding myself. Anyway, out of the Hesperus I'm pulling paras, here and there and a few new ideas. I've *got* to get this one. The strategic decision concerns the switch of centuries and I think now I'll keep it mod.

My own life has reached a new but exciting nadir. Susan is looking more than marvellous so I'm more in love with her than ever before. On the first night she banged at me with great passion about the women I have slept with and the divergence between this and my Romeo and Juliet talk to her. She told me how shocked and repelled she was and I don't think I said anything much more than 'I love you'. So we go to bed and she's suddenly fantastically passionate and soft and sweet coming two seconds after I enter. I don't come. I'm frankly bewildered. So next day I ring my mother, say 'there has been a quarrel' etc. and all looks much rosier. Then, you bet things take an ugly turn.

We have Dale and Mieke to dinner and I mention I want Mieke to take Susan on Andes cruise and I'll pay. Okay, good. Dinner goes well though Susan is annoyingly abstract. That's why we have a scrap (starting with a joke slap) in the car. This ends in tears as the foursome return here. When Mieke and Dale go I start behaving weepily. She apologizes for her earlier bloodiness, I say I love too strongly. She weeps saying I ask too much. I weep. So to bed.

Morning fuck. J. comes. Not S. I build up anger very fast.

I've lost confidence in the book. I'm crying. By bath time I'm in total collapse to my own surprise. She says it'll be all right and I keep being miserable. Honestly she seems to hold back what she wants and lets me give all. Lunch and afternoon sleep. I'm in tears again and suicidal as in the a.m. and then I get to the bottom of why. After some talk she admits she's still in contact with D. Fucked him, split, rang me in Munich, reacted, rang him, now he was to ring same place today for her to report, he and his wife now being 'separate circles which occasionally meet' – Christ – Anyway, this separate square now surfaces. Cools off quick and says, feeling control for the first time, to himself, 'joke's over now' and then goes to work on reality saying (a) Not fair this double deception, stop it. (b) Don't say you're too tired to make decisions etc. when there's one outstanding one to be made now. 'I love you.' Which I do. Entirely. I absolutely refuse Zell-am-See by which she can lay out both. She wants to see him again. So of course, falling over myself to be fair I say okay, but for the first or last time. i.e.: you don't come back if you love him. Because we've reached decision week. Now she has her breakdown. I bed children, make supper, take it up. She's constantly crying, smoking, playing pop radio. And I'm very kind, very, I think, but have to stand out now, so am sleeping alone downstairs in a short pillowed bed which accounts for this script, I'm writing on flat of my back.

One has written too many letters, sent too many telegrams, recorded in diary far too many contradictory sensations to believe in the validity of one's own thought, but whatever the result, one must continue to feel that the truth will be, is gradually being unfolded; or else the impotence of all the parties concerned and the futility of the world of love is intolerable.

Now I stick to two facts. One, Susan, Denys, David and others have insisted on the Jim/James dichotomy or schizophrenia in myself. In other words a familiar James is becoming an unfamiliar, unpredictable and unlovable Jim.

Meantime, clinical records suggest that the kind of operation Susan underwent that summer, whereby birth becomes more or less, but in practical terms, less a possibility, drives a woman to believe that she has changed. Susan's insistence that I have been transformed, or half transformed could therefore be merely a misleading but significant reflection of a truth: namely that she 'has changed'.

If this is true you have two people in early middle age at odds. One persuaded of a love for someone else, the second persuaded of the importance of his work above and beyond other human beings. And it now occurs to me that this false identity, in both cases is at the root of the problem.

I cannot remain James because however endearing James may have been he did such shoddy things, such hurtful things, such compromising things that I can no longer bear to live with him. Susan, recognizing the inadequacies of James, now that Jim has told her of these things (and other people have confirmed them), realizes that she was to some extent the fool. She cannot bear this notion and it therefore drives her further on her own divergent course. What was for her therefore a gesture of emancipation, a sense that love for David gave her a new identity, becomes a need. She feels now that she must be someone else: must prove that she is not merely the receiving end of a shoddy man. She converts this at once into terms of passion and love for a new man who has the qualities and defects utterly separate from those which have, in her mind, beleaguered her.

Both people continue to diverge yet keep harking back in a most painful manner, half loving and half hating what they have been.

The solution would seem to be to exorcize blame, because what is done cannot be undone. The double shame shows the strength of the tie. These two people's lives were ineluctably tied together. Much as they try to separate they both have a terrifying sense of their connection. They convert this into talk of children, discussion of the past moments of deception, disappointment or disillusionment.

The truth is that neither have changed. The tie is terrifying because it is reality. The two are not what they hoped they were, but if truth is to be respected they must surely recognize that this is what they were, and consequently are, and not try to get away from each other when they are in reality trying to get away from themselves. The reasons why they dislike themselves as they were, so thoroughly, are connected to James's activities: because he was unfaithful to Susan and to his mainstream work. Susan's revulsion to his extramarital sex and anti-social (i.e.: guilt of appearing as he is – a disappointment to himself) attitude drive her of course to someone who suffers neither of these defects. Nor does she wish to be associated with James's past shortcomings. But, inexorably, she is. She has something to do with them and intolerable as this thought may be, if she wants to live with reality, she must face this truth. Truth faced, that we both are the same people, but with a determination not to slide down the same road, the desperate (more than passionate) attachment to the other (who is neither weaker nor stronger, but younger) may well ease, because love is a tension. And to ease it now would seem essential unless Susan's going to do something more destructive than James has ever done, namely climb out of a screaming dilemma by involving, fundamentally falsely, another more innocent soul. The desire to get away from James is the desire to get away from life, which is to say from Susan, James's wife. To succeed in this desire is therefore not to start a new life but merely to deny a real life: to live thereafter in a play about oneself: to live no longer. David can therefore literally be said to be death for Susan as James's Proustian ambitions of withdrawal (think, in last diary) are similarly death for James. It is only together that they can live again, because the reality of the two original, wounded people is forever locked.

When I ask Susan to come back, therefore, to me, I am asking her to come back to life. I am, therefore, duty bound to fight this battle to my death – even literally to my death – or else I have made the final betrayal.

I won't betray her. I love her. I will fight.

Persuaded of my love for her, and daring for the first time to consider the possibility of her love for me I can look at my children again: dare to know my overwhelming love for them, my profound ambition for them. I become again a man with a future. Yet I tremble. All that is possibly only to say that I can't bear the thought of what I am and Susan's love seems to me, vainly, the road back to what I was. Oh misery, misery.

I feel like work, not diary, but things seem to be happening in my mind at least: I saw Susan off after good lunch at London Airport and she's carting girl children back today.

Mark Longman had some advice. First that on David's record, he reckons, there's no possibility of David dumping Ann therefore I'm right in thinking that Susan would become London mistress: and this I must stop. Second that after miserable performance over last four years (dating from Hollywood) when I've completely lost integrity as a man if not as a writer, I've played with Susan, cuckolded her, talked of it, should be utterly (and am) ashamed. I therefore have no rights whatsoever. Third, in spite of the fact that this has been an unhappy life for me, too, it's no wonder Sue chooses another man, whether it's love or passing obsession. Fourth, since crisis (and partly before) I've shown myself sick as an emotional manipulator, and used Susan as a toy. No wonder she's exhausted, I must recognize this tendency. The worst that can happen is that I'll get better. Fifth, just patience.

They're all wrong – of course, because none know this kind of love. I'll live as if it's over. That's the only way. Live as though she's dead, then when she comes in to say 'I'm going. I love him only', I'll say 'No shock, you have already gone'. Live as though she's dead. Keep her memory. Love her memory. Forget the living girl. Live and revere what was, what use to forgive? Kill the present one. Live as though she were dead. If she were dead I'd certainly set out on that contemplative work. So? So start.

You can't say it. I say too much but I can't say it. i.e.: I'm lonelier, really, I know, by far, than David. Yes, that's true. And have been, I show everything except ...

I thought she was there, that's the damn truth. I may have abused it, but I thought she was like me in this, that nothing was forbidden in love, that all could be forgiven. And I had the signs of rigidity early and ignored them. These terrible blows delivered instead of silence NEVER TO BE HURT AGAIN – She's an idiot. The opposite is true. Had she opened I'd never have had to abuse. We've shoved out feeling because we were afraid of false emotion. It's the damn *English* in the end. It really is.

Stop, stop, stop. She's gone. Weep no more. You've got one month to do the book. Do it.

Susan grew a little competitive at supper, less than loving, and I went upstairs first. Then she came to bed smiling, and I was mad: mad: I started with love, I think, but very shortly I was reeling off all the facts I've picked up from her diary etc. about 'David, you seriously expect me to take in Caravaggio when I was thinking of you all the time', of the pop tunes, of chapters there of the Orly airport on the passport. Swiftly I pieced together claiming a detective had been there, instantly denying it, mad by then and she told me she had a reply already to her letter to David i.e.: 24 hours return to her own: God knows where she picked it up ... And it was good-bye and I was mad, driving to God knows what; she ran to the garden: I called her back: I tried talk, talk, talk of my love and she was stuttering then no longer able to make sense ... And today quite drained and of course I'm trembling. Because if she cannot love me, I must kill myself. I must, lest I kill her. A victory? For me, yes, but at what cost. At such a cost that I want to give it all back to her. I want them to have each other and I can only do that by killing myself. And yet the children are very close to me. The book is emerging. If only I thought Anne could cope with me. That would be the way out.

Some Gorgeous Accident

Maybe old Fiddes never saw it himself. It has nothing to do with clearing his name. Nothing to do with having his mind made up for him, about sticking to his wife. It had to do with Link. To do with making Link feel bad about it all. Feel obligated to the doctor, that is, for the rest of his life. And Link now saw the hook.

...

'So onward, Link, and out. Drop it. To forget is to be sane. The Fiddes existed. Learn to live with that. So you loved the big idiot. Now, don't go back.'

Diary

In love returned one dares drop one's eyes: see that figure: know how it will react: invite it: lift one's eyes and ask when next? But when love is not returned the face becomes more important. One searches the face for a change – like a man looking at the clouds to see how the wind blows; to see more: to see what lies in the heavens beyond. And the clouds roll on, and on. The more one stares, sees the shape of each cloud, shape that pleases, arranges and defies memory, the less possible does it seem to be to reach the paradise beyond: the same paradise that previously was reached effortlessly by the clasp of hand.

And yet what is this paradise? Is it escape, is it the beginning or the end of imitation and of pain, or only that? Is that why we first love the young: then love our own?

The next few months, until spring 1967, are difficult to remember. What did I do? Whom did I see? I know I got thinner and spent a lot of time visiting the psychiatrist. He tried to give me back my confidence, if I ever had any. Without the children my life was totally empty, no cooking, no washing, no shopping, nothing. I can't remember. Then my father died. James came to the nursing home at Oxford; and only he and my stepmother were allowed to witness my father's end. That was my father's wish. My brother and sister and I waited outside. James was extraordinarily good. It was my first experience of death.

Diary

We've moved on now to Easter Monday. That's about the

19th April – and I'm waiting outside the private room at the Acland Home where Beryl* is with Eric, Susan's father, in what looks like the last night of his life. I never talked to him about Susan but he sent a message that he was after all a little more than 50% with me although he wished to stay neutral.

I've seen Dale: seen John: talked to Sandy, Michael Law, Mark ... received a terrible vindictive letter from Liz. All advice differs. But all ask me to have patience ... something which I haven't got. Susan and I have had some terrible rows – one over her cousin who has it in for me and from whom Susan takes advice, one over her professed lie to John that she had slept with David before the Vienna trip, one over David's last letter, which was terrible. Rolf stayed with us, didn't work hard enough, has gone home ... I'm still swaying like an old ship between the truculent and the suicidal but always I seem to love her; to want her almost unnaturally much, and she is sometimes with me, sometimes not. She's now going to a psychiatrist who pointed out that David's the kind of man who never leaves his kind of wife – a rough approximate statement I'd say – but that 'treatment' has been forestalled by the psychiatrist's other commitments. When it continues I don't know. It seems to me sometimes that Anne is the source of all this: that Susan is on an act of revenge and means to prolong it. At other times it seems to me that all, all is lost and then, for a while, I can't even write. But *Maclaren's History* does seem to be coming along. Of course I've brought in the present situation. I couldn't do anything else – and this has upset the balance of previous drafts. But it is beginning to work now, I guess.

* My stepmother

And what are these things compared to death? It's curious how small they seem, yet at the same time equally acute. I've been talking to Eric's doctor this minute and there's no question, it seems that the heart is failing – he is dying. He will not recover ... It is a question now of time. Beryl remains by his side. I wait outside. Dick's on his way.

After the funeral my brother, as executor of my father's will, gave James a pair of engraved gold cuff-links to thank him for his support. James had been fond of my father and was pleased with the present.

Because I had cried and because James had comforted me, when we buried my father's ashes at Bampton where he had been born, I returned briefly with James to the house at Fairford only a few miles away. It was the first time for so long that I had been able to feel any sort of respect for James, who managed and organized. He did not sentimentalize.

When I again returned to London by myself, he telephoned and asked me out to dinner. He was very nervous. He even rang the front door bell like a visitor. The evening was sad, subdued, but we did not quarrel. He drove me back to Highgate and we sat in the car and talked about the children. We did not make any plans. I said goodnight and he drove away. The next day he sent me a bunch of roses and signed his name 'Odysseus'. This tremulous courtship continued. We talked a lot about the white and black horses that haunted his dreams, the light and the dark side of his character. Many years before he had called me his white horse. I had often given him pale china horses, alas now all broken. He said that he didn't want to ride the black horse any more, that the events of the past few years were just beginning to drain him of those desires; though not altogether.

He went off to New York and returned without the

cuff-links, thrown, he implied, at some woman who had, to his astonishment, expected to be paid for her services.

The road back was by no means straight but since at this stage I was still seeing David, briefly and from time to time, I merely went to the jeweller's and ordered a new pair of cuff-links. On the back I had a little rearing horse engraved. He was delighted that I could joke about it, and I could only do so because I no longer felt slighted or jealous. I simply did not care. I neither loved him nor hated him, but his company was superb.

None of this new relationship was easy. His eyes, which he used to describe as currants in an unbaked bun, still blazed occasionally with sharp anger. He looked a little older and a little wiser and rather tired. His hair was beginning to go grey.

Eventually, in the spring of 1967, he asked me down to Fairford to meet his new circle of acquaintances. He took me to dinner with them and I felt like a girlfriend. We even gave a party. I was still cautious about committing myself to living with him permanently again but I was tickled by his new approach to me, the new respect, the awe.

Sadly my young stepmother, Beryl, was dying of cancer. She was only forty-three. I came back to Fairford to look after her. I could not give James much of my time as I spent most of the days with her and he consoled himself elsewhere, I don't doubt, and that was another reason why I could not sell my soul back to him again so soon.

At the end of the year he had to go back to California. He asked me to go with him. I took our son David with me and James found a wonderful apartment on the beach at Malibu. It was the sea again and a question of time. We were, surprisingly, a family. We behaved differently now. He was not particularly good or faithful and I still thought a lot about David, especially during the bad moments, but we were more adult I suppose, had a new view of each other, respected each other's secrets. I could begin to remember the dazzle of our first encounter and of that first sweet love. I found to my surprise that we had begun an equally exciting relationship, not negative and never boring.

When we returned from California I burned my boats and agreed to sell the house in London and move permanently to Fairford. We leased a small flat in an old warehouse in Soho, which we began converting into a film studio and where we planned to sleep when we were in London. James wanted to try his hand at film directing and had novels planned in his head, and occasionally on paper, that would last him into his old age. He was completing the film script for *The Battle of Britain* and we were arranging a visit to Japan. We wanted to be together, not to keep James out of trouble but because we found each other such good company. Such an up-swing. I could look at him and love him and look forward not only to the next night but to the next chapter.

We were making plans too to start that restaurant at the bottom of our garden. We even thought of starting two restaurants, on either side of the road; one to be called the Lord James and very smart, and the other to be called Jim's Inn and very cheap. One of James's new friends, Tory Lawrence, agreed to become our partner.

I arranged a dinner party so that we could meet Tory's husband, John, and discuss the project and introduce everyone to a French lady who would come and work for us. That was on December 21st, 1968. James was driving down from London and he was late. I thought, 'trouble with the police' and did not worry too much. But he usually telephoned me if he was to be late. At half past ten John telephoned the police. They said they were on their way round to see me. James had been dead since seven o'clock, but I did not believe it until

John drove me to the police station and we saw it written in the book.

Diary

She felt a kind of flurry. A kind of Yes, a scent in the May air. An edge.

A Yes, Yes: Yes! A sense the confusion is over: a clarity: the blinds closing in the cells: those definitions. Not a respect of herself. An absolute confidence in herself as a public attraction, but in the possibility of anything private.

The whole sense of a theme breaking through: of a melody that's both new and instantly recognizable: a striking of eternal links.

To Susan

Wed. 16 June '66

My darling:
You asked me very sweetly could I ever love you again after all that. I never stopped. My heart's a windmill. It flaps around: it does vulgar things; it smells a bit. But it never closed. And never will where you are concerned; never, never, never.

James
x

To Susan

L.A. 1 September '67

My Darling,
Thank you for the telegram and especially for the 'I love you' at the end. Odysseus here is continuing the script and I think it's going well. I know the novel has got further to

go than I've dared to tell myself – I looked at it last night. But really I do feel it's getting somewhere, and at the right level, too.

My cock's been a few places since you last saw it, but in male and medical hands this time. Very bewildered they've been, too; certain that it was an allergy. Anyway they gave me a soothing unguent which has proved much more successful than anything else: it covers bacteria, infections, allergies, itches, etc. The itch grew worse on your departure. We've had a boring history this way. I still rather believe that you blame me, always, for such business. You are as right to do so as I am to blame you; as this case now proves. In other words, you are wrong. This is just a kind of trial, I suppose, by the Gods. Anyway, it appears to be getting better, and by the by, to answer the (delightfully) unasked question; no, no, I have not had a 'bad' time since Munich.

Odysseus is missing home very much. I know I have to search New York for this book, maybe for the following play, but then I hope and pray that we will be all together for a little while, because there aren't, I know, so many more little whiles ahead for all of us together. I do not prognosticate particular doom; I speak of man's estate. But of all families we have the least to complain about. It has been super and with luck there are about as many years of freedom ahead as we have behind us, until Emma is 21. They've been long but wonderful years and recent storms now only mark the summer that precedes such a thunderous fall. In ten years you will be a little different to look at: very little, I guess and so long as Wasser photographs me, I won't be too bad. Odysseus feels that by packing so very much (and that implies deceptions, of course it does) into such a short time he may have gained a little in time. But were time to turn on me now, and kill me, nothing would have been lost, except the possible books and plays. I have beaten time that way. I have seen the world and my darling, you know, you don't have to be told what a massive proportion of that world (though not all of it) has been seen through your eyes. Thank you.

Have no fear. I love you too. The difficult years are behind. There remains a year or two of insistent journey and search and I know I must not avoid that – tired as I am becoming, wishing for an island for you and your children with me – and then, you wait; the triumphal march.

love,

J

Postcard to Susan from Rome

30th April, 1968

Tears, my darling, are for a life unlived, for a love unfulfilled or for a house that is not thick with voices. I begin to believe in our eternity.

x J